HOME ECONOMICS CURRICULUM ACTIVITIES KIT

HOME ECONOMICS CURRICULUM ACTIVITIES KIT

Margaret F. Campbell

Project coordinated by Dr. Robert C. Campbell

Illustrations by Diane Pastella

**THE CENTER FOR APPLIED
RESEARCH IN EDUCATION**
West Nyack, New York 10995

10 9 8 7 6 5 4 3

Library of Congress Cataloging-in-Publication Data

Campbell, Margaret F.
    Home economics curriculum activities kit / Margaret F. Campbell.
Illustrations by Diane Pastella.
        p.   cm.
    ISBN 0-87628-400-4
    1. Home economics—Study and teaching.   I. Title.
TX165.C33   1990
640′.71—dc20   90-42598
                                                                            CIP

ISBN 0-87628-400-4

THE CENTER FOR APPLIED
RESEARCH IN EDUCATION
BUSINESS & PROFESSIONAL DIVISION
A division of Simon & Schuster
West Nyack, New York 10995

Printed in the United States of America

ABOUT THE AUTHOR

Margaret F. Campbell, a graduate of The Pennsylvania State University, has taught home economics for over 15 years. She is currently Home Economics Coordinator in the State College Area School District, State College, Pennsylvania where she has had extensive experience in curriculum development and staff training. She was selected "Pennsylvania Home Economics Teacher of the Year" in 1984.

Mrs. Campbell has also been an associate in Educational Computer Consultants since 1983 and has conducted many computer education workshops to train staff in the use of computers in education.

She is a coauthor of *Computer Literacy Activities Kit: Levels I and II* (Prentice Hall, 1987) and *Computer Applications Activities Kit: Ready-to-Use Lessons & Worksheets for Secondary Students* (Prentice Hall, 1989).

ABOUT THIS BOOK

The *Home Economics Curriculum Activities Kit* presents step-by-step directions for preparing and teaching over thirty stimulating enrichment lessons to students in grades 7–12. The detailed lesson plans will quickly build your knowledge of content and teaching techniques if you are a beginning home economics teacher. If you are an experienced home economics teacher, you will find that this book adds depth and interest to your repertoire.

The lessons encompass four of the major areas of home economics: (1) Foods and Nutrition, (2) Human Growth and Development, (3) Management and Consumerism, and (4) Textiles and Clothing. Although the lessons in each section are arranged in sequence, most need not be taught that way. The kit can serve as a core of experiences for a complete general home economics course at either the junior or senior high school level. You may also pick and choose from these lessons to enhance your existing program.

HOW TO USE THIS BOOK

For easy use, the lessons in *Home Economics Curriculum Activities Kit* have been standardized. The lesson format is as follows:

- *Concepts*: This is a list of the concepts taught in the lesson.
- *Objectives*: This is a list of the student objectives to be achieved in the lesson.
- *Teacher Preparation*: Here are the detailed steps you need to take to prepare yourself to teach the lesson—from brushing up your knowledge to making copies of student activity sheets to purchasing needed supplies.
- *Activities*: This is a chronological list of activities, complete with step-by-step procedures, for teaching the lesson.
- *Background Information*: Many lessons contain supplementary information about the content that may help you better understand the ideas presented. Extension activities and optional approaches to the lesson are frequently discussed.

Each lesson is then followed by the full-page, ready-to-use activity sheets you and your students will need for that lesson. These can be reproduced as many times as necessary for use by your students.

You will find that the following procedures for using the book will work well in your daily preparation:

1. Read through the entire plan for the lesson. Make sure you fully understand the purpose of the lesson. The lessons in this book call for the practice of higher-level learning skills. They require students to analyze, synthesize, and apply the knowledge contained in the lesson.

2. Match the items under "Teacher Preparation" with the classroom activities described in the "Activities" section. Complete each teacher-preparation activity to the degree you feel necessary to teach the lesson comfortably.

3. Collect and prepare the materials needed for the lesson. Arrange them in the sequence they will be used during the lesson.

4. Use your standard procedure to prepare for the classroom presentation as outlined under "Activities."

A special feature of *Home Economics Curriculum Activities Kit* are the appendices, which contain blackline masters for transparencies and answer keys to the activity sheets.

OTHER THINGS YOU NEED TO KNOW

Several of the lessons suggest the use of microcomputers and suggested software. Although these are not required, they are recommended. Home economists have always been at the forefront of technology in the home and should, therefore, be making use of learning technology in their classrooms.

Suggestions are given throughout the book of sources to write for free and inexpensive materials that students can use in the lesson. It is a good idea to go through the book immediately and order the materials so that you will have them in ample time.

Several of the lessons suggest how to involve the entire school in the activities. This is an excellent way to spread the word about how vital and interesting home economics really is. It is the only subject in the school curriculum that teaches life skills in any sort of organized sequence. It is your responsibility to see that as many students as possible take advantage of what you have to offer.

KNOWLEDGE AND SKILLS

This book is based upon a body of knowledge and a set of skills familiar to most home economists.

- *Foods and Nutrition*: This area prepares individuals to understand the principles of nutrition; the relationship of nutrition to health and well being; the selection, preparation, and care of food; meal management to meet individual and family food needs and patterns of living; good economics and ecology; and the optimal use of the food dollar.

- *Human Growth and Development*: This area prepares individuals to understand the nature, function, and significance of human relationships within the family and with other individuals. It includes instruction in the uniqueness of families and individuals, the development and socialization of the individual, and meeting the needs and interests of individuals and family members.

- *Management and Consumerism*: This area prepares individuals to understand the values, needs, wants, goals, and resources that enable individuals to make rational decisions and to understand the establishment and maintenance of a satisfying home and family life.

● *Textiles and Clothing*: This area prepares individuals to understand the social, psychological, and physiological aspects of clothing and textiles; the nature, acquisition, and use of clothing and textile products; the selection, construction, maintenance, and alteration of clothing and textile products; and the effect of consumer choices on the individual and family as well as the clothing and textile industries.

A FINAL WORD

The *Home Economics Curriculum Activities Kit*—complete with lesson plans, reproducible activity sheets, transparency masters, and answer keys—contains everything you need to successfully teach your students much of the knowledge and many of the basic life skills they will need later in life. Home economists play a key role in the education of our young people. I wish you success in using these lessons to help prepare your students for successful daily living in the 21st century!

Margaret F. Campbell

CONTENTS

HUMAN GROWTH AND DEVELOPMENT • 71

MANAGEMENT AND CONSUMERISM • 123

TEXTILES AND CLOTHING ● 173

FOODS AND NUTRITION

■ KITCHEN SAFETY

CONCEPTS

- Knowledge of safety procedures helps to prevent accidents in the kitchen.
- Safety techniques should be practiced when cooking.
- Knowledge of what to do in case of an accident in the kitchen is important.

OBJECTIVES

The student will:

- determine the proper procedure to use in a given set of kitchen safety problems
- practice the rules of good safety during laboratory sessions
- complete a safety quiz

TEACHER PREPARATION

- Make copies of the safety situation scenario cards found in Appendix A.
- Make enough copies of "Kitchen Safety Quiz" and the activity sheet "Safety" for each student.
- Select a kitchen safety resource book to be used by students who are unable independently to solve the safety problems.

ACTIVITIES

1. Introduce this lesson by discussing safety in the kitchen. Is the kitchen the type of environment where safety should be a concern? Why? Is it analogous to working on an assembly line? How? What kinds of things are present in a kitchen to make it hazardous? What type of accidents could occur in a kitchen? What steps can be taken to prevent accidents? Distribute the activity sheet "Safety." Explain to students that they will be working in small groups to propose solutions to hypothetical safety problems around a kitchen. They will be given a safety situation card. The group should discuss the problem and pose at least one solution to each question. Have each group choose an official recorder and a spokesperson. The recorder is responsible for the final

wording of the group's solution and the spokesperson will orally present the group's report to the class.

Assign the students to groups and indicate the amount of time they have to complete the task. You may wish to circulate around the room and assist those groups who may be experiencing difficulty.

2. Have each group make a brief report to the class about the problem and the group's solution. As the groups give their solutions, try to get at the ''why'' of the decision.

3. Administer the ''Kitchen Safety Quiz.''

4. Conclude the lesson by discussing the following questions:
   a. Why do accidents occur in kitchens?
   b. How can most kitchen accidents be avoided?
   c. Who is responsible for a safe kitchen environment?

Name _____   Date _____

SAFETY

Situation number: _____   Group number: _____

PROPOSED SOLUTION

_____
_____
_____
_____
_____

NOTES

_____
_____
_____
_____
_____
_____
_____
_____
_____
_____
_____

KITCHEN SAFETY QUIZ

We have been discussing the importance of kitchen safety. By following some simple rules and practicing some common sense procedures, we can make our kitchen a safe place in which to work. Remember, a safe environment can save you from a lot of painful accidents.

DIRECTIONS: Complete the following sentences to find out how much of a safety expert you already are!

1. When handling a hot pan or dish, always use a _____
   _____

2. When boiling water is to be poured into a glass measuring cup, place the cup on a tray in case the _____
   _____

3 Handles of pans and skillets should be turned _____
   _____ the range.

4. To remove food from the oven, you should first _____
   _____

5 To avoid bumping into cupboard doors and drawers, _____
   _____

6. When using sharp knives, you should cut in the direction _____
   _____

7. If you break a glass, use a dust pan and brush to pick up the large pieces and _____ to pick up the small pieces of glass.

8. Never connect the current of an electric appliance when your hands are _____

9. When you climb, use a _____

■ SANITATION SAVVY

CONCEPTS

- All food preparation and clean-up activities contribute to kitchen sanitation.
- Prepared foods should be both wholesome and uncontaminated.
- Food prepared under unsanitary conditions can cause food poisoning.
- Food poisoning is dangerous.
- Food should be stored properly to prevent unwanted growth of bacteria that leads to food poisoning.

OBJECTIVES

The student will:

- define bacteria
- know the optimal temperature at which bacteria grows
- demonstrate proper sanitation practices when preparing recipes in the food laboratory
- conduct an experiment to observe bacterial growth

TEACHER PREPARATION

- Prepare copies of the activity sheets "Sanitation Savvy," "The Facts Are," "Experiment," "Don't Be a Statistic," and "Sanitation Facts." Each student will need two copies of "Experiment."
- Review the Background Information section of this lesson.
- Complete "Sanitation Facts" and have the answers ready for easy reference.
- Obtain copies of free booklets about food safety, such as *The Safe Food Book* (#534P) and *Safe Food to Go* (#597P), both published by the Consumer Information Center, Department MM, Pueblo, CO 81009. Allow four to six weeks for delivery.
- Obtain eight petri dishes, sterilized nutrient agar jell, and a wax pencil. Your science department probably has these items.
- Prepare 3″ x 5″ cards to use during the activity "Experiment." The cards should contain the following information:

1. Use a wax pencil to divide the petri dish into four quadrants by drawing lines on the bottom of the dish.
2. Use only three quadrants. The fourth will serve as your control. DO NOT TOUCH IT!
3. Complete the group assignment for the three test quadrants.

● Divide the class into groups of four students.

ACTIVITIES

Class Period 1

1. Introduce this lesson by having students read and discuss the information contained in the activity sheet "Sanitation Savvy." Ask students if any of them has ever had food poisoning. What were their symptoms? Does food poisoning occur frequently? Are some food poisoning symptoms mild?
2. Direct the students to study the chart "The Facts Are." Review this information so that students learn what causes food poisoning, how it occurs, its symptoms, and how to prevent it.

Class Period 2

Begin this class by explaining that students will be conducting an experiment to discover personally the conditions under which harmful bacteria grow. Have the class break up into groups of four. Distribute the 3″ x 5″ cards.

Group 1:

a. Press back of clean spoon in one section.
b. Lick spoon, and press it into another section.
c. Drop a clean spoon on floor, and press it into a third section.
d. Place lid on dish, label, and place in kitchen cabinet.
e. Repeat process with a second dish and place in the refrigerator.

Group 2:

a. Press unwashed finger in one section.
b. Wash hands with soap and water. Dry. Press finger in a second section.
c. Blow nose into tissue. Do not wash hands. Press finger in the third section.
d. Place lid on dish, label, and place in kitchen cabinet.
e. Repeat process with a second dish and place in refrigerator.

Group 3:

a. Press a section of a clean, wet dishcloth in one section.
b. Wipe the inside of the sink and counter with a cloth and press into a second section.
c. Wash hands, and dry on a clean dish towel. Press a damp section into a third section.
d. Place lid on dish, label, and place in kitchen cabinet.
e. Repeat process with a second dish and place in refrigerator.

Group 4:

a. Press a fresh piece of luncheon meat, handled with a fork, into the first section.
b. Press a second piece of luncheon meat, which has been left at room temperature, into a second section.
c. Use your hands to press a fresh piece of luncheon meat into the third section.
d. Place lid on dish, label, and place in kitchen cabinet.
e. Repeat process with a second dish and place in refrigerator.

Class Period 3

In three to five days, check the petri dishes to see if they are ready to be evaluated. When they are ready, have the students complete "Experiment." All students should examine all dishes. Finish the lesson by discussing each group's findings and summarizing at the chalkboard or an overhead projector, the conditions under which bacteria grow. Have students generate a list of *do's* and *don'ts* regarding care and handling of foodstuffs.

Class Period 4

1. Discuss the concepts found in Background Information to have students learn how to prevent food poisoning. The discussion should touch on such questions as the following: What are the causes of food poisoning? Why do people eat food that is not fit for consumption? How can food poisoning be prevented? How do you know if you have been poisoned by food? Have students complete the activity sheet "Don't Be a Statistic" after the discussion.
2. Distribute the activity sheet "Sanitation Facts." Have the students write in the answers as you discuss the contents of the fact sheet. The fact sheet is based upon information from USDA Food Safety Inspection Service, Food and Drug Administration Consumer Services, and Centers for Disease Control. If you need additional information, consult these sources.

BACKGROUND INFORMATION

Every year, 100 million people get ill from food that has spoiled because of improper handling and storage. Their illness is caused by one of the high-risk bacteria that routinely are found in our food supply. The symptoms of these illnesses range from simple flatulence and cramps to death.

Most food poisoning is the result of human error. You can protect yourself if you know the basics of food sanitation. Everybody shares in the blame—from homemakers to food processors, preparers, and servers. Fifty percent of all food-borne disease comes from meals eaten at home, and fifty percent from meals eaten out.

Why do people eat food that is not fit for consumption? The pathogenic and toxigenic organisms that can be found in food are often silent killers because their presence cannot be detected by taste, appearance, or odor. Illness may be the only clue that food is spoiled.

Food-borne illness can most easily be prevented by controlling the growth of bacteria through temperature control. Most bacteria are destroyed when the temperature exceeds 165°F and is prevented from growing if the temperature exceeds 140°F or falls below 40°F. The danger zone is the zone between these extremes. Keep food at a temperature outside this zone, and you can stop worrying about your next meal being your last! Bacteria multiplies slowly while in the food, but once inside the body, its growth rate explodes.

In addition to cooking and storing food at the proper temperature, the cooking environment should also be kept clean. This includes both cooking equipment and the persons doing the food preparation. Handwashing is particularly important after going to the bathroom.

SANITATION SAVVY

The kitchen is your workplace when you engage in food preparation in the home. Just like the factory and the office, personal work habits and environmental conditions affect the final product. In the case of your kitchen, they determine whether the food you prepare will be free from harmful bacteria.

Your personal work habits should be considered first. Always wash your hands with hot water and soap before handling food. Dry them on a towel reserved for that purpose. Never touch your hair, tissues, or handkerchief without rewashing your hands. Do not put your dish towel over your shoulders, use it to wipe up spills, or wipe your hands. Always rewash any food that drops on the floor if you intend to use it. Use a separate spoon each time you taste the food you are preparing. If you leave the kitchen to do something else, always wash your hands before continuing with your food preparation. Fruits and vegetables to be used in cooking should be thoroughly washed.

The degree of environmental sanitation is determined by the cleanliness of the work areas, appliances, utensils, and kitchen area at large. Always use clean utensils and a clean working surface. When washing dishes and utensils by hand, add a measured amount of detergent to a sink one-third full of hot water. Wash least-soiled items first, rinse with hot water, dry if necessary, and return to storage promptly. When using a dishwasher, follow the manufacturer's directions. Use a damp cloth to wipe countertops, stove, and other appliances. Leave the sink clean and dry. The floors, walls, and cabinets should be kept free from grease and other dirt. Trash cans should be emptied before dishes are washed.

Food is easily contaminated by careless handling during preparation and storage. This frequently leads to—

FOOD POISONING!
What is it?
What causes it?
What will it do to you?
How can it be prevented?

THE FACTS ARE

Bacteria	How it Occurs	Symptoms	Prevention
Staphylococcus Aureus (Staph)	Spreads from contaminated food handler; found on skin, in cuts and scrapes, pimples, and throat infections of food handler.	2 to 20 hours after eating, vomiting and diarrhea may start; lasts 1 or 2 days.	Be especially careful when handling ham and other meat, poultry, tuna and poultry salads, cheeses, egg products, starchy salads made with mayonnaise (potato, macaroni, pasta), custards, and cream-filled desserts.
Salmonella	Occurs when contaminated meat, poultry, eggs, and fish are eaten raw or undercooked; when served food comes in contact with contaminated food; or when infected person contaminates food.	6 to 48 hours after eating, diarrhea, fever, and vomiting can occur; may last 2 to 7 days. Infants and children are at greatest risk.	Keep raw food away from cooked food. Thoroughly cook meat, poultry, and fish. Be especially careful with poultry, pork, roast beef, and hamburger. Don't drink unpasteurized milk. Don't use counters, cutting boards, or utensils that come in contact with raw meat or other foods until they have been washed.
Clostridium Perfringens	"Buffet" germ that grows rapidly in large portions of food—often roast beef and turkey cooling slowly. Also occurs in chafing dishes that may not keep food hot enough and in refrigerators if food is in large portions and does not cool quickly.	8 to 24 hours after eating, diarrhea, gas pains may start; ends in less than a day. Older persons and ulcer patients are at great risk.	Keep food hot (over 140°F) or cold (under 40°F). Divide bulk foods into smaller portions for serving and cooling. Be careful with poultry, gravy, stews, and casseroles.
Campylobacter Jejuni	Occurs in raw milk or untreated water, or when a pet becomes infected and spreads it to family, or when raw or undercooked meat, poultry or shellfish is eaten.	2 to 10 days after eating, severe diarrhea (possibly bloody), cramping, fever, and headache occur; may last 2 to 7 days.	Don't drink untreated water or raw, unpasteurized milk. Thoroughly cook meat, poultry, and fish.
Clostridium Botulism	Usually occurs in home-canned or any canned goods showing warning signs—clear liquids turned milky, cracked jars, loose lids, swollen or dented cans or lids. There is not always a bad odor.	12 to 48 hours after eating, nervous system could be affected. Symptoms of botulism include double vision, droopy eyelids, trouble with speaking and swallowing, and difficult breathing. Untreated botulism can be fatal.	Carefully examine home-canned goods before use. Beware of any jar or can that spurts liquid, has swollen or dented sides or lids, or has an odor when opened. Don't store cooked foods at room temperature.

Name _____   Date _____

EXPERIMENT

PROBLEM: Food can become poisonous due to growth of dangerous bacteria.

HYPOTHESIS: Improper care and handling of food and failure to follow principles of good sanitation can lead to the growth of bacteria.

OBSERVATIONS: Identify the contents of each quadrant on the line provided. Draw a picture or describe the results in each quadrant.

At Room Temperature

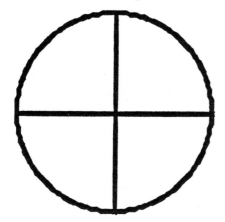

Refrigerated at 40°F

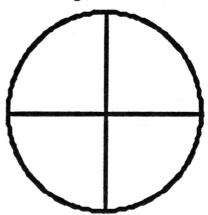

CONCLUSIONS

1. The hypothesis is correct. _____ Why? _____

_____

2. The hypothesis is incorrect. _____ Why? _____

_____

3. List three rules of good sanitation that can be supported by your findings:

   a. _____

   b. _____

   c. _____

DON'T BE A STATISTIC

1. What is bacteria? _____

_____

_____

_____

2. At what temperature is bacteria killed? _____

3. At what temperature is the growth of bacteria retarded?

_____

4. What causes food spoilage? _____

5. Why do so many people become ill from eating spoiled food? _____

_____

_____

6. In addition to proper cooking and storing, list two other rules for good food sanitation. _____

_____

_____

_____

7. Do more people get ill from eating out or at home? _____

8. How many high-risk bacteria can be found in food? _____

9. Name three bacteria found in food. _____

_____

_____

10. How does food poisoning affect us? _____

_____

_____

_____

_____

_____

_____

_____

_____

SANITATION FACTS

1. Cooked turkey allowed to sit at room temperature is the number one source of salmonellosis. True
   _____ False _____

2. Most foods are unsafe for human consumption when moldy.

   True _____ False _____

3. There are three ways to safely thaw frozen meat or poultry. Should you: (a) refrigerate overnight; (b) use the microwave; (c) put the meat or poultry in a watertight plastic bag and immerse in cold water, changing the water often; (d) all of the above? Circle the correct answer.

4. What is the only way to kill the 150 strains of salmonella bacteria that affect humans? _____

5. How is the last date a food product should be used identified on the package? _____

   _____

6. What are the safest foods to take on a picnic? _____

   _____

   _____

7. The two highest-risk cleaning supplies in the home kitchen are the sponge and dish cloths. True
   _____ False _____

8. What foods other than dairy products, meats, fish, and poultry are most likely to have salmonella

   contamination? _____

   _____

9. The term "sell by" on a food product label indicates the last day on which a product should be sold. Is it safe to use the product two or three days after that date?

   _____

10. What should you do with melted ice cream? _____

    _____

(continued)

SANITATION FACTS (continued)

11. Why shouldn't fruit or vegetable juice be refrigerated in open cans? Circle the correct answer: (a) salmonella toxins can breed; (b) vitamin C is lost; (c) lead leaches into the juices; (d) all of the above.

12. The ideal refrigerator temperature is: (a) 40°F; (b) 20°F; (c) 10°F. Circle the correct answer.

13. How long will the following foods keep at a temperature of 40°F:

    (a) oysters _____; (b) pork _____; (c) raw eggs _____;

    (d) lettuce _____; (e) cottage cheese _____.

14. How long will perishable foods keep safely in the refrigerator in case of a power failure? _____

15. A food freezer should be kept at:
    (a) −10°F; (b) 0°F; (c) 10°F. Circle the correct answer.

16. Which of these foods will last a year without refrigeration? (a) canned vegetables; (b) cereals; (c) raisins; (d) non-fat dry milk; (e) dried fruit; (f) soup; (g) bouillon products. Circle the correct answer.

17. Tuna and cooked eggs spoil rapidly and should never be used in outdoor meals.

    True _____   False _____

18. What are the two best ways to avoid botulism? _____

    _____

    _____

19. Why is it risky to sniff moldy foodstuff? _____

    _____

20. Butter, animal fat drippings like bacon, and margarine—if tightly wrapped or covered—are safe for

    30 days in the refrigerator. True _____   False _____

© 1990 by The Center for Applied Research in Education

■ MEASURING TECHNIQUES

CONCEPTS

- Accurate measuring is essential to proper food preparation.

OBJECTIVES

The student will:

- observe a demonstration of measuring techniques
- successfully complete the activity sheet "A Measure of Success"
- use proper measuring skills while preparing Cranberry Mist

TEACHER PREPARATION

- Select several frequently measured ingredients (salt, flour, sugar, vanilla, brown sugar, milk, etc.) and organize them for students to practice measuring.
- Purchase ingredients for the Cranberry Mist recipe.
- Assign students to work in groups if this has not been done previously.
- Prepare copies of the activity sheets for this lesson.

ACTIVITIES

1. Ask if anyone knows who decided how large a cup should be or how long a yard should measure. Has anyone heard the nursery rhyme "Jack and Jill"? Does anyone know the origin of the rhyme? If so, have that student tell it to the class. If not, relate the story about it found under Background Information. Conclude the story by stressing the need for accuracy in measuring.

2. Explain that a recipe, no matter how good it is, cannot overcome the careless habit of measuring improperly. Each ingredient is used for a special reason. Measurements must be level and exact for the final product to be satisfactory. Ask students if they have ever prepared a recipe, not measured accurately, and the recipe still seemed to work? Why do they believe the product was satisfactory?

3. Demonstrate how to measure each ingredient you have selected. Ask students how they would measure an ingredient before you demonstrate measuring it. Students often have a store of knowledge in the foods area. This is a time to let them shine!

4. Distribute the activity sheet "Measure of Success" and have students write the answers to questions 1, 2, and 3. Read through the directions and complete questions 4 and 5.

5. To practice measuring accurately, have the students prepare the recipe for Cranberry Mist. Explain any rules that you want students to follow during the preparation. Point out the location of the special pieces of equipment needed to complete the assignment. Circulate around the lab offering assistance to students who need help.

6. After the students have had a chance to taste the Cranberry Mist, ask them to evaluate their cooking experience. Use the activity sheet "Did I Measure Up?"

BACKGROUND INFORMATION

Almost every nation in the world uses a system of measurement based on the distance between the equator and the North Pole. In one country, however, the measuring system is based on the arm length of a 16th-century queen! Surprisingly, the country that uses such an old-fashioned system is, perhaps, the most technologically advanced nation in the world—the United States.

Our system of measurement can be traced back even further than the 16th century. More than 3,500 years ago, the Egyptians devised a system that used parts of the human body to measure length, width, and volume. The foot was the length of an adult human foot. The distance from the tip of the middle finger to the elbow was called a cubit. Two cubits made one arm, also called a yard. Amounts of food and liquids were measured by using the term *ro,* which was equal to one mouthful.

The drawback to such a system is obvious. The sizes of human body parts differ from person to person. Therefore, an amount of food or the length of something being measured could be very different lengths depending upon whose foot or arm was being used as the measuring device. However, this disadvantage did not prevent the system from spreading to ancient Greece, Rome, and throughout all of Europe.

In England during the middle ages, the *ro* was used to measure food and liquids. A new measurement was created by doubling the *ro.* It was called a handful. Two handfuls were a jack, and two jacks a jill. A jill could be doubled to make a cup. Two cups make a pint, and two pints make a quart.

The demand for a more accurate system came in the 1600's during the reign of Charles I in England. Charles decided to take advantage of the unequal measurements by placing a tax on everything sold by the jack. In addition, he decreased the size of a jack. The peasants were hardest hit by this action. Since they had little money, they typically bought their food in small amounts, usually no more than a jack of milk or a jill of grain, for example. Charles's action made the peasants pay more money for less food. The jack, then later the jill, became unpopular with the peasants. Eventually, the jack and jill went out of favor.

The peasants celebrated the end of the use of the jack and jill by making up a rhyme that survives to this day: "Jack and Jill went up the hill to fetch a pail of water. Jack fell down and broke his crown, and Jill came tumbling after."

In time, a standard set of measurements was agreed upon. It is known as the English system of measurement.

The French, in the meantime, were developing what they considered a better system of measurement. In the 1700's, they calculated the distance from the North Pole to the equator. They called one ten-millionth of that distance a meter. This is the basis of the metric system. The United States is the only major country in the world that has not adopted this system of measurement.

A MEASURE OF SUCCESS

1. What is the correct procedure for measuring liquids?

   a. _____

   b. _____

   c. _____

2 What is the correct procedure for measuring dry ingredients?

   a. _____

   b. _____

   c. _____

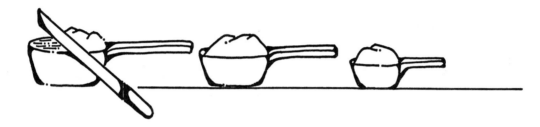

3. Which ingredients are sifted, and why? _____

   _____

   _____

   _____

   _____

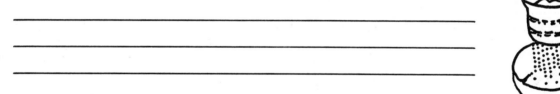

4. Read through the recipe listed below and place an ''L'' beside the liquid ingredients, a ''D'' beside the dry ingredients, and an ''H'' beside ingredients that we use our hands to measure.

Cranberry Mist

Combine in a saucepan:

_____ 1 cup cranberry juice

_____ 1¾ cups water

_____ ½ stick cinnamon

_____ 2 whole cloves

(continued)

A MEASURE OF SUCCESS (continued)

Bring the mixture to a boil and then remove it from the heat.
Remove spices with a slotted spoon.

Then add and mix well:
_____ ¼ cup frozen lemonade concentrate
_____ 2 tablespoons sugar

Reheat and serve.

EQUIPMENT NEEDED: _____

_____

_____

_____

MY JOB(S): _____

_____

_____

_____

5. When cooking is a group activity, the tasks to be completed need to be divided equally among the group members. Look at the Cranberry Mist recipe and divide the jobs so that everyone in the group has one. List your job in the space above. Also, list all of the equipment you will need.

Preparing this recipe will give you practice measuring and using the stove. You will also learn the location of the equipment in your kitchen.

Remember to assign someone the job of setting the table!

GOOD LUCK!

© 1990 by The Center for Applied Research in Education

Name _____   Date _____

DID I MEASURE UP?

Kitchen number: _____

Evaluation Checklist	Excellent	Good	Needs Improvement
1. I practiced proper sanitary procedures.			
2. The people in my kitchen worked well together.			
3. The proper equipment was used.			
4. The recipe was correctly followed.			
5. Each person did his or her job.			
6. The kitchen was cleaned at the end of the period.			
7. I was aware of others' safety.			
8. I used safe personal habits.			
9. The ingredients were measured correctly.			
10. The recipe was followed exactly.			
11. The product tasted tart and tangy.			
12. The product looked good.			

TEACHER COMMENTS: _____

_____

_____

The grade I feel I earned is _____ because _____

_____

_____

_____

_____

_____

_____

■ TOOLS OF THE TRADE

CONCEPTS

- Kitchen utensils are important to food preparation.
- Selection of the proper utensils contributes to ease of preparation.
- Use of the proper utensils may improve the quality of the product.

OBJECTIVES

The student will:

- identify tools needed for general food preparation
- use required tools to complete a given recipe
- assess how the use of proper tools eases preparation tasks and contributes to better product quality

TEACHER PREPARATION

- Make copies of the activity sheets "Tools of the Trade," "Muffins," and "Muffin Scorecard."
- Have samples of the 25 utensils to be identified.
- Purchase the ingredients needed to prepare the muffins.
- Have class textbooks for students to use to complete "Tools of the Trade."
- If you have not already done so, divide the class into appropriate kitchen groups.
- Arrange to use three class periods for this lesson.

ACTIVITIES

Class Period 1

1. Introduce this lesson by pointing out that, like many other activities, food preparation requires some basic tools. Ask why this is so. Explain that students are to use one of the reference books you have provided to complete the activity sheet "Tools of the Trade."
2. When everyone has finished this task, go over the answers, show them the utensils, and describe their functions.

Class Periods 2 and 3

1. Following this activity, provide students the opportunity to use the utensils. Distribute the recipe for the muffins. Have students get into their kitchen groups and make a list of the utensils needed to prepare the recipe. Have them make a second list for the ingredients needed. Have a spokesperson from a volunteer kitchen read the first list to the class. Make any necessary additions or deletions. Have a student from another kitchen do the same for the ingredients list.

2. Explain that students are to divide the recipe tasks and get organized to prepare the muffins. Who is going to do what? Review how to use a recipe. Stress the importance of accurate measuring and correct use of each utensil.

3. When the muffins are in the ovens, discuss the characteristic of a good muffin. You may wish to go over each item on the "Muffin Scorecard."

4. Have each kitchen rate its muffins and share the results with the class.

5. Close this lesson by discussing such questions as the following: Which utensils made preparing the muffins easier? Why? Which utensils were absolutely necessary to prepare the muffins? Why? Which of the utensils are used in preparing many types of recipes? Would they put them on a list of basic tools needed in every kitchen? Why? Are there tools that can be substituted for each other? What are they?

TOOLS OF THE TRADE

Using the correct cooking utensil is important. Each piece of equipment has a specific function in the preparation process. Proper use of cooking utensils affects the use of time and energy, and leads to a good product.

Label each utensil and write a brief description of its use.

1. _____ is used to

   _____

   _____

2. _____ is used to

   _____

   _____

3. _____ is used to

   _____

   _____

4. _____ is used to

   _____

   _____

5. _____ is used to

   _____

   _____

6. _____ is used to

   _____

   _____

7. _____ is used to

   _____

   _____

8. _____ is used to

   _____

   _____

(continued)

TOOLS OF THE TRADE (continued)

9.

_____ is used to

_____

_____

10.

_____ is used to

_____

_____

11.

_____ is used to

_____

_____

12.

_____ is used to

_____

_____

13.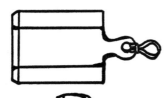

_____ is used to

_____

_____

14.

_____ is used to

_____

_____

15.

_____ is used to

_____

_____

(continued)

TOOLS OF THE TRADE (continued)

16. _____ is used to

_____

_____

17.  _____ is used to

_____

_____

18. _____ is used to

_____

_____

19.  _____ is used to

_____

_____

20. _____ is used to

_____

_____

21.  _____ is used to

_____

_____

22. _____ is used to

_____

_____

© 1990 by The Center for Applied Research in Education

(continued)

TOOLS OF THE TRADE (continued)

23.

_____ is used to

_____

_____

24.

_____ is used to

_____

_____

25.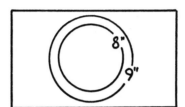

_____ is used to

_____

_____

MUFFINS

Here is a recipe for Whole Wheat Muffins from *The American Heart Association Cookbook*, Fourth Edition (New York: Ballantine, 1984):

    1 cup whole wheat flour
    1 cup sifted all-purpose flour
    ½ teaspoon salt
    2½ teaspoons baking powder
    3 tablespoons sugar
    1 egg (or egg whites or egg substitute equivalent to 1 egg)
    1 cup skim milk
    ½ cup oil

    Grease muffin tins lightly with oil.
    Sift the two kinds of flour together with the salt, baking powder, and sugar.
    Add the egg, milk, and oil. Stir quickly until only barely blended. Do not beat.
    Fill each muffin tin ⅔ full of batter. Bake at 425°F for 20 to 25 minutes.
    YIELD: twelve 2¼-inch muffins
    APPROXIMATE CALORIES PER SERVING: 175

The utensils needed are: _____

_____

_____

_____

_____

My jobs are: _____

_____

_____

_____

MUFFIN SCORECARD

Use the following key to rate the muffins:

Excellent = 4   Good = 3   Fair = 2   Poor = 1

APPEARANCE

Golden brown, nicely rounded top, pebbly, not smooth; creamy white inside.

_____ Excellent   *Note*: If poor, you probably overmixed or
_____ Good   your oven temperature was not correct.
_____ Fair
_____ Poor

TENDERNESS

Breaks easily without crumbling; light and tender.

_____ Excellent   *Note*: If poor, you probably overmixed or
_____ Good   used too much flour.
_____ Fair
_____ Poor

TEXTURE

Uniform medium texture; slightly moist; free from tunnels.

_____ Excellent   *Note*: If poor, you baked too long, or the
_____ Good   temperature was too high, or you used too
_____ Fair   much flour. If tunnels appeared, you
_____ Poor   overmixed.

FLAVOR

Delicate; slightly sweet.

_____ Excellent   *Note*: If poor, you used old or
_____ Good   poor-quality ingredients.
_____ Fair
_____ Poor

OVERALL EVALUATION: _____ (total points)
If you got a 16, you're a
star muffin maker! That's
perfect!

29

■ RECIPES

CONCEPTS

- A recipe is a guide for food preparation.
- An exactly followed recipe guarantees the success of food preparation.

OBJECTIVES

The student will:

- study the information on the activity sheet "Recipes"
- complete the activity sheet "Recipes Are Necessary"
- plan, prepare, and evaluate "Super Biscuits"

TEACHER PREPARATION

- Prepare copies of the activity sheets "Recipes," "Recipes Are Necessary," "Super Biscuits," and "What Did You Score?"
- Purchase the ingredients to prepare the biscuits.
- Organize the ingredients on trays for each kitchen.

ACTIVITIES

1. Begin this lesson by reminding students that in the two previous lessons, they prepared two food products, Cranberry Mist and Muffins. Both of these turned out to be delicious. Ask them what they did that assured their success. They will give several answers: measured accurately, used the right ingredients, followed a set of directions, and so on. Point out that all of these helped make the final product good. The task for today is to analyze why, and how, the recipe was, and is, always so very important.
2. Distribute the activity sheets "Recipe" and "Recipes Are Necessary." Have students read the information, answer the questions, and discuss their answers.
3. Thoroughly review the biscuit recipe with the class. Ask students to divide the jobs, list the utensils needed, check the students' planning, and prepare the product. Assist those students experiencing difficulty.

30

4. When the biscuits are out of the oven and ready to be evaluated, have the students use ''What Did You Score'' to evaluate their product.

5. Conclude this lesson by asking questions about the recipe and its parts. Be sure to include:
    a. What are the two parts of a recipe? (list of ingredients and procedure)
    b. List the important information that the recipe provides. (ingredients, amounts, procedure, cooking time and temperature, amount recipe makes, specialized equipment needed)

RECIPES

A recipe is a set of instructions or a guide to help you prepare food. Always read through the entire recipe to get an overall idea of what is to be done. Make it a practice to start a recipe only when you are sure of each step. If you are uncertain or confused about anything, refer to the special terms section of a cookbook or ask someone for help.

The information below will help you understand how best to use a recipe for guaranteed results!

PREPARATION FOR COOKING

Read through the entire recipe with special care. Carry out all of the steps one-by-one in the order given:

1. Assemble the ingredients
   a. Note carefully the quantities you need.
   b. Focus on the abbreviations. Make sure you know what they mean.
   c. Check your understanding of the cooking terms used in the recipe (dice, mix, etc.). These are the keys to success!
2. Get the necessary utensils ready for use.
3. Preheat the oven to the required temperature.
4. Measure the ingredients as exactly as a pharmacist measures the ingredients in a prescription.

METHOD

Carry out all of the steps one-by-one in the order given:

1. Watch for special action words, such as . . .

sift	blend	grease
cream	chill	slice
beat	preheat	cool

2. Perform these techniques correctly! Remember that even though some words seem to differ slightly (dice, mince), there is a decided difference in the action required to complete them.
3. Reread the directions, review the cooking terms, or ask for help if you don't understand the directions.
4. Mix carefully. Carry out each step with care!
5. Bake and time precisely.

© 1990 by The Center for Applied Research in Education

Name _____   Date _____

RECIPES ARE NECESSARY

1. List the important reasons for using a recipe to prepare foods.

   _____

   _____

   _____

2. Why should you read the entire recipe before beginning?

   _____

   _____

   _____

3. A recipe has two important parts. What are they?

   a. _____

   b. _____

4. What are "action" words?

   _____

   _____

   _____

   _____

5. Circle the "action" words in the recipe "Super Biscuits."

6. How can "action" words help you determine the utensils needed to prepare a recipe?

   _____

   _____

   _____

7. Perhaps you know someone who cooks without using a recipe. List the circumstances under which such a person might not need a recipe to be a successful cook.

   _____

   _____

   _____

   _____

   _____

   _____

Name _____   Date _____

SUPER BISCUITS

BEFORE YOU START

Read the recipe carefully.
Assemble the ingredients.
Collect the utensils needed.
Preheat the oven.

INGREDIENTS

2 cups sifted flour
3 teaspoons baking powder
1 teaspoon salt
⅓ cup shortening
1 cup skim milk

PROCEDURE

1. Preheat the oven to 450°F.
2. Mix the sifted flour, baking powder, and salt together in a bowl.
3. Cut in shortening with a pastry blender until mixture resembles coarse corn meal.
4. Add skim milk and stir until blended. DO NOT OVERMIX.
5. Drop from a tablespoon onto a lightly greased baking sheet.
6. Bake at 450°F for 10 to 12 minutes.
7. Remove from sheet. Serve at once.

LIST THE UTENSILS NEEDED

_____

_____

_____

_____

MY JOB IS

_____

_____

© 1990 by The Center for Applied Research in Education

Name _____   Date _____

WHAT DID YOU SCORE?

Name of recipe: _____

Names of judges: _____

OUTSIDE CHARACTERISTICS

Shape: nicely rounded
Texture: crisp with a rough surface
Color: uniform
Size: 1½ the size of unbaked biscuits

GOOD 3 points	FAIR 2 points	POOR 1 point

INSIDE CHARACTERISTICS

Color: creamy white; free from yellow
       or brown spots
Grain: flaky, pulling off in thin
       sheets; medium fine, even cells

Texture: tender; slightly moist; light
Flavor: pleasing; well-blended with no
       bitterness

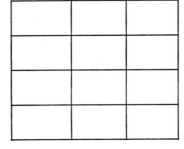

35

■ MICROWAVE MAGIC

CONCEPTS

- Microwave cooking is convenient and fast.
- The microwave oven uses a different set of heating principles than a conventional oven.

OBJECTIVES

The student will:

- describe the principles of microwave cooking
- use appropriate techniques when cooking in a microwave oven
- evaluate the advantages and disadvantages of microwave cooking

TEACHER PREPARATION

- Make copies of the activity sheets "Microwave Magic," "Microwave Puzzle," "Where Is It Hottest?" "Microwave vs. Conventional Cooking," and "Microwave vs. Conventional Cooking Scorecard."
- Select a recipe to demonstrate microwave cooking principles.
- Collect the necessary ingredients and utensils needed to prepare the noted recipe and menus.
- Plan several simple, appealing and nutritious menus for students to use to evaluate microwave vs. conventional cooking.
- Have a thermometer and liquid measuring cups available to demonstrate the cooking temperatures of different mixtures.

ACTIVITIES

Class Period 1

1. Begin this lesson by asking students how many of them have microwave ovens at home and what foods are prepared in them. Follow this by asking them to explain how microwave energy works.

36

2. Have the students complete the activity sheet "Microwave Magic" while you discuss the content contained in the Background Information.

3. Have students complete the "Microwave Puzzle." Discuss the answers and summarize the general microwave concepts to conclude this part of the lesson.

4. Show the students appropriate utensils for use in a microwave oven (plastic, glass, paper towels, etc.). Distribute the activity sheet "Where Is It Hottest?" Explain that you are going to demonstrate something about the way heating takes place in a microwave oven that is very important for them to know. Place an equal amount of water at the same temperature in five different measuring cups in five different locations as shown in the diagram on the activity sheet. Heat the water, take the temperatures, and have the students write them in the spaces provided on the activity sheet. Ask the students what they observed about the temperature of the water in the measuring cups. Correct! They are different! What does that tell them about the way microwave heat is distributed? Give them a few minutes to think about what conclusion(s) they should have reached that they will need to apply to microwave cooking. After a few minutes, ask for examples of conclusions. The conclusion is they will need to stir or rotate food being cooked in a microwave oven if it is to be properly prepared.

5. It is also important students know that foods with sugar or fat heat more quickly. Add sugar to one container of water, some cooking oil to another, and water to another. Heat them and take their temperatures. Give students some time to consider the results. Ask them what this indicates about the cooking time of solutions high in fat or sugar. (They will require less cooking time.)

Class Period 2

1. It is important for students to understand that they must follow basic food preparation principles if they are to be successful. They also need to know that there are some differences between microwave and conventional cooking. Chief among these is the concept of "standing" cooking time in the microwave oven. To bring these ideas home, prepare a batch of Raspberry Tart Squares.

   As you prepare the recipe, discuss the basic food preparation principles, which are the same for both types of cooking; for example, accurate measuring of ingredients, correctly following the steps of the recipe, and so on.

   Point out to students that there is a process called "standing time" in microwave cooking. That is, food continues to cook after it is removed from the microwave oven. Therefore, it is important to provide for this if hard, overcooked, dry food is to be avoided. The standing times are given in the general or introductory sections of a microwave cookbook as well as in the book that accompanies the microwave oven when purchased.

   Here is the recipe for Raspberry Tart Squares from *The Microwave Guide and Cookbook* (Consumer Information Testing Laboratory, 1983):

Raspberry Tart Squares
POWER LEVEL: High (10)
MICROWAVE TIME: 8 to 10 minutes, total
¾ cup butter
1 cup brown sugar

1½ cups unsifted all-purpose flour
1 teaspoon baking powder
½ teaspoon salt
1½ cups quick-cooking oatmeal
1 cup finely chopped pecans
1 12-ounce jar raspberry jam

In 12″ × 8″ × 2″ dish, place butter. Microwave at High (10) for 1 to 1½ minutes, until melted. Stir in brown sugar, flour, baking powder, salt, oatmeal, and pecans; blend well. Remove half of crumb mixture to bowl or wax paper. Pat remaining crumbs evenly over bottom of dish.
Cover patted-out crumbs with raspberry jam and sprinkle with remaining crumbs over top.
Microwave at High (10) for 7 to 9 minutes, rotating dish a half turn after 4 minutes.
Recipe makes about 30 squares.

2. While the squares are baking, tell the students they are going to prepare a simple menu, using both a conventional and a microwave oven. They will evaluate both methods using a scorecard after they have completed preparing and sampling the menu.

Keep the menu plan simple at this stage. Something like the following would be appropriate:

Breakfast	*Lunch*
Oatmeal with Raisins	Bean Taco
Whole Wheat Toast	Vanilla Pudding
Hot Chocolate	OR
OR	Pita Pizza
French Toast	Vegetable Soup
Applesauce	Fresh Fruit
Cranberry Tea	

Divide the class into four groups. Group 1 will prepare breakfast using the microwave oven while Group 2 will use a conventional stove. Group 3 will prepare lunch using the microwave oven and Group 4 will use a conventional stove. Have the students get into the groups to begin to organize their lab procedures. Have them complete the activity "Microwave vs. Conventional Cooking."

3. When the Raspberry Tart Squares have completed the time necessary for baking in the microwave oven, get the students' attention. Show them that the bars are underbaked and do not look as attractive as they should. Let the students go back to their planning and, after the proper amount of standing time, get their attention again and show them that the bars are completely baked and look more appetizing. Let the students sample the squares. How would they describe their quality? What rating would they give the quality? Why?

Bring this lesson to an end by briefly reviewing the need to follow basic food preparation principles and the standing time principle for microwave cooking. Remind students that tomorrow they will be contrasting microwave and conventional cooking in the preparation of a menu for breakfast or lunch.

Class Period 3

1. Begin the lesson by asking students questions to review basic food preparation principles, standing time, reading a recipe, etc. Review any special lab procedures you want them to follow. Make sure they understand they will need to keep a record of how long it took them to prepare the items on the menu and how long it took to cook the items on the menu. Describe the evaluation procedure and go over the activity sheet they will use.

2. After the food has been prepared, have the students sample each menu and complete the "Microwave vs. Conventional Cooking Scorecard." When the students have completed their scorecards, and their evaluations have been discussed, conclude this lesson by asking: What are the differences between microwave and conventional cooking? What are the advantages of each method of cooking? What are some considerations you must make when converting a conventional recipe for use in a microwave? Other than cooking method, what factors influenced your scoring? Which method of cooking is better? Why?

BACKGROUND INFORMATION

Microwaves are a form of electromagnetic energy much like that of heat, light, or radio waves. A magnatron tube within the oven produces the microwaves and a fan distributes them throughout the oven. The waves penetrate the food and cause the molecules (a minute particle, smallest portion of an element or compound that retains chemical identity with the substance in mass) of the food to vibrate rapidly, thus creating heat. This acts in the same way as rubbing your hands together to cause heat. Simply, a microwave oven is a device that produces electromagnetic energy that is converted to heat when it is absorbed by the food placed in the oven.

The cooking time in a microwave oven is determined by starting temperature, the volume of food, the density, the moisture content, and the shape of the food. Density refers to lightness, firmness, or porous nature of the substance. Microwaves penetrate dense substances more slowly; therefore, cooking time needs to be increased. Likewise, foods with high water content require more energy to reach the desired temperature. Foodstuff with relatively high fat and sugar contents come to temperature quickly in a microwave oven. For example, the frosting on a cupcake will become hot before the cupcake itself, meat closest to the fat will heat first, and so on.

The shape of the food influences the cooking time. Flat, thin food articles heat faster than thick, large pieces. Try to keep pieces of food the same size for even heating. When possible, arrange food into a round shape. This avoids overcooking on the edges. Stirring will help to redistribute the heat within some foods. Another technique is to rearrange the food in the oven. Turning the food or repositioning it is done when stirring is not possible. Covering the food helps to retain steam and to speed cooking. It will also help prevent spattering and dehydration.

Food will continue to cook when it is removed from the microwave oven. It is necessary, therefore, to provide standing time. This is especially necessary for large pieces of dense foods.

Some important facts about microwave cooking to remember are the following:

1. Pierce whole fruits or vegetables to allow steam to escape.
2. Do not cook eggs in the shell. Pierce the yolk with the tip of a fork before cooking.
3. Pierce or open plastic lids or other airtight containers to allow steam to escape.

4. Liquids should be stirred or poured just before heating to avoid eruption.

5. If foods begin to smoke or burn, turn off oven and extinguish the fire.

6. Do not use containers with restricted openings, such as baby food jars or catsup bottles, because of rapid expansion.

7. Do not pop regular popcorn. Use microwave-ready popcorn only.

8. Do not use metal cookware because sparks (arcing) will occur.

9. Do not can foods in a microwave oven. The metal lids interfere with uniform heating of food in jars and lead to food spoilage.

10. Do not use newspapers and recycled paper in a microwave oven because they can burn.

To adapt your favorite recipe for use in the microwave oven, study the recipe. Is it a food that microwaves well? Look for cooking techniques that are similar to microwave techniques, such as covering, steaming, or cooking in sauce or liquid. If the food requires a crisp crust or very dry surface, it may be better to cook it conventionally. Since liquids do not evaporate when microwaved, reduce the amount in saucy casseroles. Add more thickening to sauces and gravies. Reduce some seasonings; they will not lose intensity in the short time required for microwave cooking. Salt meat and vegetables after cooking. If an ingredient takes longer to microwave than others in the same dish, precook that ingredient before adding it to the dish.

An excellent videotape, called *Microwave Secrets*, discusses these concepts. It is available from Sharp Electronic Corporation, Sharp Plaza, Mahwah, NJ 07430.

MICROWAVE MAGIC

If you like your food in a hurry, using a microwave oven may become your preferred method of cooking.

1. What are microwaves? _____

_____

_____

_____

2. What is a molecule? _____

3. What is density? _____

4. How does microwave energy cook food quickly? _____

_____

_____

5. In addition to your oven's power, what other factors influence cooking time?

_____

_____

_____

6. List facts to remember when cooking with a microwave oven.

_____

_____

_____

_____

7. List guidelines to follow when adjusting a conventional recipe for the microwave oven.

_____

_____

_____

_____

_____

_____

MICROWAVE PUZZLE

ACROSS

2. Breaking the skin or membrane of foods or a plastic bag to allow steam to escape
5. Cooking food to less-than-done stage
7. Any dish or container to hold food in a microwave oven
10. Inverted cover or dish to hold food above the cooking liquids
11. Turning over a food during cooking

DOWN

1. Foods cooked too long, dried out, hard spots, etc.
3. Spark caused by discharge of static electricity in a microwave oven
4. Time required to heat or cook foods to serving temperature (two words)
6. Outer surface or skin breaks from the buildup of steam
8. Time suggested to allow heat to spread to center of food
9. Turning container or food a quarter to a half turn for more even cooking

© 1990 by The Center for Applied Research in Education

WHERE IS IT HOTTEST?

Cup 1   Cup 2

Cup 3

Cup 4   Cup 5

CONCLUSION:

_____

_____

_____

_____

_____

sugar   fat   plain water

CONCLUSION:

_____

_____

_____

_____

MICROWAVE VS. CONVENTIONAL COOKING

MENU PLAN:

1. _____

2. _____

3. _____

4. _____

Cooking method: _____

List of ingredients needed:

_____

_____

_____

_____

_____

_____

_____

Menu

Appetizers

Onion Soup
Soup du Jour
Salad

Entrees

Broiled Trout
Steak Diane
Cajun Chicken
Filet Mignon
Oriental Shrimp

Beverages

Soda Water
Wine
Coffee
Tea
Milk
Soft Drinks

Desserts

Fruit Cup
Pecan Pie
Chocolate Mousse

© 1990 by The Center for Applied Research in Education

List of utensils needed:

_____

_____

_____

My jobs are:

_____

_____

_____

Name _____   Date _____

MICROWAVE VS. CONVENTIONAL COOKING
SCORECARD

1. Menu: _____   Cooking method: _____

   Preparation time: _____

   Cooking time: _____

2. Menu: _____   Cooking method: _____

   Preparation time: _____

   Cooking time: _____

3. Menu: _____   Cooking method: _____

   Preparation time: _____

   Cooking time: _____

4. Menu: _____   Cooking method: _____

   Preparation time: _____

   Cooking time: _____

SCORECARD

KEY: 1 = poor   2 = fair   3 = satisfactory   4 = good   5 = excellent

	Menu 1	Menu 2	Menu 3	Menu 4
Appearance	● 1 2 3 4 5	● 1 2 3 4 5	● 1 2 3 4 5	● 1 2 3 4 5 ●
Color	● 1 2 3 4 5	● 1 2 3 4 5	● 1 2 3 4 5	● 1 2 3 4 5 ●
Texture	● 1 2 3 4 5	● 1 2 3 4 5	● 1 2 3 4 5	● 1 2 3 4 5 ●
Flavor	● 1 2 3 4 5	● 1 2 3 4 5	● 1 2 3 4 5	● 1 2 3 4 5 ●
Ease of Preparation	● 1 2 3 4 5	● 1 2 3 4 5	● 1 2 3 4 5	● 1 2 3 4 5 ●
TOTAL SCORE	●	●	●	● ●

AND THE WINNER IS _____!

45

■ IT'S CONVENIENT

CONCEPTS

- Use of convenience foods may shorten the time it takes to prepare meals.
- Personal management, skill, and cost influence the selection of convenience foods.
- Food additives are substances added to food products to maintain or improve nutritional value, to maintain freshness, to assist processing, or to make it more appealing.
- Convenience foods are usually more expensive than their fresh counterpart.
- Convenience foods are often less nutritious than their fresh counterpart.

OBJECTIVES

The student will:

- learn the definition of convenience foods and food additives
- be able to identify additives on a food product label
- be introduced to the process used to compare convenience foods and food prepared from scratch for time of preparation, energy used, cost, quality, nutritive value, appearance, and skill required
- assess those circumstances when the use of convenience food products may be the most cost effective approach to food preparation

TEACHER PREPARATION

- Select a variety of convenience items to be discussed in class. Include representatives from fresh, canned, frozen, dehydrated, partially prepared, ready-to-serve, and packaged dry mixes.
- Review your basic knowledge about convenience foods. See the Background Information.
- Have copies of a nutrient chart available for students to complete the activity sheet "Compare."
- Select recipes to prepare products from scratch and selected convenience products for use in a comparison lab.
- Assemble the necessary ingredients and convenience products for the comparison lab.
- Prepare a list of the prices paid for the ingredients and products.
- Make copies of the activity sheets "Technology Strikes Again," "I Wonder What It Is," and "Compare."

46

ACTIVITIES

Class Period 1

1. Arrange the selected convenience food products in a display easily observed by the class. Ask the students if they know what these kinds of food products are called.

2. Discuss convenience food products. Be sure to include such information as the following: the factors that make a food product a convenience item; the different forms in which convenience foods can be purchased; criteria to consider when making a decision to use a convenience product or prepare something from scratch; the quality, cost, and nutritional value of convenience foods; and basic principles of food preparation needed in preparing convenience foods.

3. Distribute representative samples of convenience foods to each table. Have the students read the labels and make a list of any ingredient with which they are not familiar. Have them record their findings on "I Wonder What It Is." When everyone has finished, compile a class list at the overhead projector or chalkboard. Have students study the list to see if they can surmise that many of the items are food additives. Point out that it is important they know something about food additives. They have played a key role in the development of the convenience food industry.

4. Move into a discussion of the information that answers the questions found in the activity sheet "Technology Strikes Again!" It is important students know what a food additive is, why they are added to food, the advantages and disadvantages of additives, and why consumers should be knowledgeable about food additives.

5. Conclude this lesson by asking the following questions: Under what conditions would you choose to use a convenience food instead of preparing it from scratch? What are the advantages of convenience foods? Disadvantages? Why are convenience foods generally more costly? What are some of the reasons the number of convenience foods has increased so dramatically?

   Consumers are faced daily with making choices about what food to prepare. In the next lesson, you will do some judging about convenience vs. home-prepared food.

Class Periods 2 and 3

1. Introduce the lesson by pointing out some of the conditions/circumstances that can dictate whether or not convenience foods are chosen for a meal. The purpose of this lesson is to provide students with some rudimentary skills/evidence as to why and when convenience foods are chosen. They will be conducting a comparison lab test. Have them get organized into their lab teams according to your usual procedure. Note that for this lab you will need five kitchens.

2. Stress the importance of team work, careful reading of the recipe, use of proper utensils, and accurate timing and temperature. It is essential that students keep a very accurate record of the time needed from start to finish. Have them divide the tasks in each recipe so that all tasks are completed within the lab period.

3. Make group assignments:
   Group 1—homemade vanilla pudding and instant vanilla pudding
   Group 2—fresh green vegetable and its frozen counterpart
   Group 3—homemade chili and a boxed chili mix

Group 4—homemade cornbread and packaged cornbread mix
Group 5—homemade cream of mushroom soup and canned cream of mushroom soup

4. Designate the time allowed to complete the tasks.

5. Review the activity sheet "Compare," making sure students know how to complete the taste test. Explain that they are to label each product with time for preparation, nutrient value, and whether it is homemade or a convenience food. The nutrient values for convenience foods are usually found on the label and homemade items should be based on the nutrient chart you have provided each kitchen. (If a food is not found on a nutrient chart, you need to compile it from ingredients listed.)

6. Circulate throughout the lab and give assistance where it is needed.

7. Evaluate and score products using the activity sheet "Compare." You may want to make a transparency of the sheet and complete a tally of the individual scores at the overhead projector.

8. Bring this lesson to a close by discussing the questions at the end of "Compare."

BACKGROUND INFORMATION

The supermarket is a jungle of boxes, jars, cans, bottles, fresh and frozen foods, and delicatessen items. The task of preparing meals each day has changed for many families due to the introduction of convenience foods and microwave ovens. Bread was the first convenience food, and later canned goods and packaged cereals were introduced.

A convenience food is food that has been processed or prepared to eliminate part of the preparation required for cooking or when part of the cooking has already been done. Convenience foods can be purchased in several forms: fresh, canned, frozen, dehydrated, partially prepared, ready-to-serve, and as packaged dry mixes.

Some points to consider when you are deciding to use a convenience food are time, energy, cost, quality, nutritive value, and your skill in food preparation. The price of convenience foods includes the cost of the food plus the cost of processing, packaging, labor and management, shipping, and marketing. Some convenience foods may cost the same or more than home-prepared foods; however, the difference in cost may be made up by the smaller amount of time spent in the kitchen. Some convenience foods are often better in taste and appearance than a homemade product made by an inexperienced person. Basic cooking principles cannot be ignored when you are using convenience food products. Convenience foods save the time of assembling, measuring, and mixing ingredients. However, they have not eliminated the need for learning the basic principles and the correct techniques and skills of basic cookery. Directions must be followed carefully. Generally speaking, convenience foods are higher in salt, fat and calories, and lower in fiber and trace minerals than their homemade counterparts.

Convenience foods often have serious nutritional disadvantages. This is not to say they should not be used, but their drawbacks should always be considered. See Scholastic's *Choices* magazine, pages 24–27, April 1989, for an interesting summary of homemade and convenience food comparisons.

Many new foods were made possible through the use of food additives. These are ingredients that are added during preparation, processing, or packaging. Their purpose is to improve or protect flavor, color, and texture of the foodstuff; to retain its nutritional value; or to increase shelf life.

Most foods that are needed for good health are highly perishable. Meat, milk, fruit and vegetables—unless they are frozen, dehydrated, or preserved by some other technique—spoil quickly. Food additives are used extensively to preserve these foods. There is controversy over the number of food additives a person should ingest. Consumers are asking which additives may be harmful, how many are too many, and are they really needed? To protect the health of consumers, their use is controlled by the Federal Food and Drug Administration (FDA).

Some key points about food additives are the following:

- Food additives have been used for centuries.

- Additives allow for a longer shelf life of many food products.

- Additives used for appeal purposes only are unnecessary. They add nothing to the nutritional value of the food and some may, in fact, be unsafe for human consumption.

- Manufacturers attempt to sell their products by making them more colorful and flavorful through the use of additives.

- Additives that have been used for years have been found to be unsafe or of questionable safety. Some examples are Red Color #2, #3, and #40; carbon black, cyclamates, saccharin, and sodium nitrate.

- Additives can improve the texture, flavor, and appeal of food.

TECHNOLOGY STRIKES AGAIN!

1. What are convenience foods?

_____

_____

_____

2. Identify the forms in which convenience foods can be purchased.

_____

_____

_____

_____

3. What are food additives?

_____

_____

_____

4. Why are additives added to food?

_____

_____

_____

5. Are food additives safe?

_____

_____

_____

(continued)

© 1990 by The Center for Applied Research in Education

Name _____   Date _____

TECHNOLOGY STRIKES AGAIN! (continued)

6. What points should you consider when deciding to use a convenience food?

_____

_____

_____

_____

7. What factors contribute to the cost of convenience foods?

_____

_____

_____

_____

8. When is convenience worth the extra cost?

_____

_____

_____

_____

9. Why must basic food preparation principles to adhered to when preparing convenience food products?

_____

_____

_____

_____

Name _____

Date _____

I WONDER WHAT IT IS

Carefully examine the list of ingredients on each food product. List those that you cannot correctly identify.

INGREDIENT	PURPOSE
1. _____	_____
2. _____	_____
3. _____	_____
4. _____	_____
5. _____	_____
6. _____	_____
7. _____	_____
8. _____	_____
9. _____	_____
10. _____	_____
11. _____	_____
12. _____	_____
13. _____	_____
14. _____	_____
15. _____	_____
16. _____	_____

Cake Mix Ingredients

sugar, enriched bleached flour (enriched with iron and the vitamins niacin, thiamine mononitrate, riboflavin), vegetable shortening (partially hydrogenated soybean oil), leavening (baking soda, mono-calcium phosphate, sodium aluminum phosphate, and dicalcium phosphate) to make cake rise, propylene glycol monoesters (for smooth texture), dextrose, salt, polyglycerol esters (for smooth texture), cellulose gum (for smooth batter), xanthum gum (for smooth batter), ascorbic acid (to protect freshness), modified food starch, soy protein isolate, FD&C Yellow No. 5, artificial coloring and flavoring

Nutrition Information
(per serving)
12 servings per container
serving size 1/12 cake

Cake	Mix	Baked
Calories	190	260
Protein (g)	2	3
Carbohydrates (g)	36	36
Fat (g)	4	11
Sodium (mg)	270	285
(615 mg/100 g mix)		

52

Name _____   Date _____

COMPARE

Your task is to evaluate each food product the class has prepared. Be an individual. You know what you like.

After carefully examining and tasting each product that has been prepared, enter your rating in the appropriate block.

The rating system to use for Flavor/texture, Nutritive value, and Appearance is: 5 = GOOD, 3 = FAIR, 1 = POOR. The rating system to use for Time, Cost, and Skill is: 5 = LEAST, 3 = MODERATE, 1 = MOST.

Product	A	B	C	D	E	F	G	H	I	J
Time										
Cost										
Flavor/texture										
Nutritive value										
Skill										
Appearance										
TOTAL SCORE										

Product A: canned, cooked convenience, or instant pudding
Product B: homemade vanilla pudding
Product C: fresh green vegetable
Product D: frozen or canned green vegetable
Product E: homemade chili
Product F: boxed chili mix
Product G: canned cream of mushroom soup
Product H: homemade cream of mushroom soup
Product I: homemade cornbread
Product J: cornbread mix

(continued)

COMPARE (continued)

1. What factors influence food choices?

   _____

   _____

   _____

2. How has the use of convenience foods revolutionized meal preparation?

   _____

   _____

   _____

3. Why can it be difficult to compare prepared foods with homemade products?

   _____

   _____

   _____

4. List four basic food preparation principles you must follow to prepare convenience foods.

   _____

   _____

   _____

5. List three factors that influence the decision to use a convenience vs. a home-prepared product.

   _____

   _____

   _____

© 1990 by The Center for Applied Research in Education

■ PERSONAL NUTRITION

CONCEPTS

- Calories are used by the body for physical activity and basal metabolism.
- Knowledge about the function of nutrients in the body and the amounts needed daily can affect personal dietary choices.
- Knowledge of myths about nutrition leads to better diet planning.

OBJECTIVES

The student will:

- determine the number of calories needed for a given sex, age, and metabolic activity level
- identify the six classifications of nutrients, their food sources, and their function in the body
- complete an analysis of foods consumed in a 24-hour period by using a dietary analysis computer software program
- evaluate his or her personal diet and determine changes needed
- learn about selected myths in nutrition

TEACHER PREPARATION

- Make copies of the "Eat Smart," "Nutrient Knowledge," "Personal Energy Estimate," "Dietary Recall," "Diet Evaluation," and "Menu Plan" activity sheets.
- Arrange for a microcomputer system complete with printer to be available for classroom use or a visit to your school's computer lab.
- Have available your regular classroom textbooks so that students will have nutrient information and food sources charts to use.
- Obtain several resources, such as *Food Values of Portions Commonly Used* by Pennington and Church (New York: Harper & Row, 1989) or *Nutritive Value of Foods* (USDA, 1981).
- Have several calculators available for student use.
- Schedule students' computer time. See information under Class Period 4.

ACTIVITIES

Class Period 1

1. To introduce this lesson, ask questions such as the following: How many of you looked in a mirror this morning? If you did, does that suggest you must be concerned about how you look? How many believe a person's appearance is influenced by what he or she eats? Do you want to have enough energy to get through the day with ease or do you want to have life be a drag? Do you want to have fun, be filled with energy, be able to play sports? Conclude the discussion by pointing out that from their responses, it is obvious they need to be interested in nutrition. Point out that during the next several class periods, the lessons will focus on their personal nutrition habits. They will have the opportunity to complete a personal inventory and make decisions regarding any changes that may be necessary.

2. Have the students read the activity sheet "Eat Smart." Discuss this information.

3. Distribute the activity sheet "Personal Energy Estimate." Demonstrate how students are to complete this sheet by completing an example for a hypothetical person. For example, have them read the introduction section. Discuss and clarify the different parts of the process. Next, have them complete the Frame Size section. Move on to the Age, Height, Weight section. Show them how to extrapolate this data and use the frame size information to calculate their "ideal" weight. For example, if a person is taller than 5'5", then add five pounds for every inch over 5'5". If a person is shorter than 5'0", then subtract five pounds for every inch under 5'0". It is important that students recognize that bone (frame) size should influence body weight. Persons with small bone structure should weigh less than persons with large bone structures.

   This discussion leads nicely into the next step, which is looking at basal metabolism and specific energy needs.

4. Discuss the section of the activity sheet related to basal metabolism. Plan to define basal metabolism and discuss how it affects energy consumption and body weight. Have students locate the basal metabolism calories they burn per day.

   To complete this sheet, students will have to know how to read the body surface chart and be able to determine activity levels. For body surface, students need to know approximately how much they weigh and how tall they are. Have them put a dot on the chart beside their height and one beside their weight. Use a straight edge to draw a line to connect the dots. The point where the line goes through the center column on the body surface chart is the student's body surface in square meters. This number is used to help determine basal metabolism.

   People also burn calories by being physically active. The more active a person is, the more calories he or she will burn. Briefly discuss energy output so that students will be able to determine if they are sedentary, light, moderate, or very active. For example, you could state that if a person simply goes to school, returns home, and sits around watching television or doing homework, he or she would be considered sedentary. Light activity involves going to school and then engaging in some sort of physical activity such as washing dishes, cleaning a room, or going for a walk. Students who are moderately active participate in a planned athletic activity after school such as dancing, tennis, ice skating, and so on. A very active person is one who engages in very strenuous work or who is in physical training.

5. Bring this lesson to a close by discussing such questions as the following: Are the number of calories we eat each day the only important measure of good health? What other dietary needs should we consider? Is food the only consideration for healthy living? It is important that students understand how frame size, age/height/weight, and basal metabolism influence personal nutrition decisions. Be sure to point out that the use of this process only gives a rough estimate of an individual's calorie need.

6. Briefly review the next steps in the process of determining personal nutrition needs.

Class Period 2

1. The purpose of today's lesson is to get students thinking about nutrients: (1) they are needed by the body, (b) if an individual nutrient is missing in a diet for an extended period, the function of that nutrient will not be performed, and (c) over time, being poorly nourished leads to poor health and low energy. Have students complete "Nutrient Knowledge" using a resource you have provided. Discuss the information after the chart is completed. It is important to do this before the students have the computer analyze their diet so they do not become overanxious when messages such as "You are a candidate for a heart attack" might appear on the monitor.

2. Briefly review the next steps in the process of determining personal nutrition needs.

Class Period 3

1. Now that the students know the specific number of calories they need each day, they need to determine if they are being well-nourished. Distribute the sheet "Dietary Recall" and explain how the students are to complete it. Point out that it is essential to list EVERYTHING they ate during the 24-hour period they are assessing, including all those little tastes of food offered by others, the quick cookie on the way through the kitchen—EVERYTHING!

   Caution students to try to be specific and list the amounts of food eaten in measurable terms, such as 1 ounce or ½ cup. You can assist students with this by showing them what an ounce of cereal looks like or describing a serving size from each of the four food groups. Remind students to list beverages, condiments, candy, and the like.

2. After students complete their list, ask them if they experienced any difficulty remembering everything they ate. Why do they think this was so? We are barraged daily with opportunities to consume food! Did they eat about what they would have guessed? More? Less? Why do dieters write down what they eat immediately following consumption? It is because memory can't be trusted, and all those calories add up! Conclude the discussion by reviewing why it is important for individuals having a weight or nutrition problem to keep accurate records.

3. Demonstrate how to use the computer and the dietary analysis software students will use to complete their personal analysis. Take this opportunity to point out some of the advantages of using a computer—its speed and accuracy vs. using nutrient charts and having to make calculations by hand, for example. Inform the students about any codes required by the computer software. For example, in *Eats*, you need to look up a number code for each food eaten and type that into the computer rather than typing in just the name of the food.

   The amount of time you spend on this activity will depend upon the amount of experience the students have had with the computer. You might let students assist you by entering information, printing a hard copy, and so forth.

4. Conclude this lesson by informing students about the procedure that will be used to complete their individual computer analysis. For example, the next class period will be held in the computer lab, or students will work in pairs at the computers in the classroom, and so on.

Class Period 4

1. The approach used for this class period will depend upon whether you have one or two computers in your classroom or you have access to a computer lab in the school.

   If you have access to a computer lab, the approach is very straightforward. Take students to the lab and have them complete the analysis using the software you provide.

   If you have only one or two computers, assign students to teams of two or three, and give them a specific time to complete the analysis while the rest of the class is completing their private assessment and making decisions about any changes they may need to make.

   The activity could also be modified to complete several samples as a large group.

2. Review again what constitutes a healthy diet. Explain the Basic Four Food Groups and the number of servings needed daily by a typical teenager.

3. Have the students complete their dietary analysis.

4. When the students have a copy of their dietary analysis, have them evaluate it to determine if any dietary changes are required. You may wish to suggest a procedure. For example, have them code each food they ate by assigning it to one of the Basic Four Food Groups. Then check it against the recommended allotment: Bread and Cereal—4 servings of 1 ounce or piece per day; Vegetables and Fruit—4 servings of ½ cup or 1 piece per day; Milk and Dairy—4 servings of one 8-ounce glass or 1 ounce cheese per day; Meat and Poultry—two 3-ounce servings (for a total of 6 ounces) per day. Have students complete the activity sheet "Diet Evaluation."

5. It is important that students know how to apply their knowledge. Distribute the activity sheet "Menu Plan" and have them prepare a daily menu for a typical teenager. The menu should provide food that is attractive, tasty, and contains the proper number of nutrients and calories. When the students have completed this task, ask for volunteers to share their menus with the class and lead a discussion to determine if they are correct.

6. Conclude the lesson by reviewing the factors that make up sound personal nutrition. Point out how they contribute to making a person look and feel good physically. Encourage them to consider making any modifications that seem to be needed based upon their personal analysis. What positive benefits might they expect to achieve? Why is it important not to make any drastic changes in a diet plan after monitoring only one 24-hour period? Why do most weight-loss diets suggest consulting a physician before making dietary changes?

Class Period 5

1. Nutrition is frequently discussed in the media by people who are either trying to lose weight or "muscle up" for a sport. These people may or may not be experts. Students pick up ideas about

nutrition that may be myths rather than facts. To enlighten students about some of these myths, have them play "Nutrition Trivia."

Form the students into teams of three or four. The task is to answer the question based upon the team's thinking. One person should be designated as the spokesperson for the team. One point is given for each correct answer. If a team is unable to answer the question correctly within a brief time span, about five seconds, call upon another team. No point is awarded in this instance. The team with the most points is the "Nutrition Trivia" winner.

Nutrition Trivia Questions

Will eating carrots help you see in the dark? (**No, not unless you are deficient in vitamin A. It helps with eye adjustment and may help you see in dim light.**)

Is brown bread better for you than white bread? (**Yes, there are more fiber, vitamin B$_6$, and trace minerals in brown bread.**)

Does spinach make you strong? (**No, not any stronger than other green leafy vegetables.**)

Does an apple a day keep the doctor away? (**No, it does not contain much vitamin C, only two grams of fiber, and 50 calories.**)

Does chocolate cause acne? (**No, active endocrine glands do. If you think a food is causing excess oil in your skin, eliminate that food for several weeks to see if there is an improvement in your skin's condition.**)

Can you sweat off fat? (**No, perspiration is water.**)

Do oranges or other vitamin C rich foods prevent colds? (**No, although there is some evidence this vitamin will reduce the severity of a cold.**)

Do protein supplements help build muscles? (**No, muscle is 22% protein and 70% water, so extra dietary protein doesn't help; exercise instead.**)

Are crash diets a good way to lose weight? (**No, most crash diets produce a water loss and do not promote healthy eating habits.**)

Does a candy bar give you quick energy? (**Yes, initially, but it can later make the blood sugar drop because there is an increase in insulin.**)

Can vitamin and mineral supplements safely be used in place of food? (**No, they don't supply protein, carbohydrates, fat, fiber, or some trace minerals.**)

Is it possible to take too much vitamin C? (**Yes, too much can produce kidney stones.**)

Cholesterol is found only in foods of animal origin. True or false. (**True**)

Standing erect burns more calories than sitting. True or false. (**True**)

If an ingredient label doesn't say sugar, then the product doesn't contain any. True or false. (**False. Dextrose, glucose, fructose, maltose, lactose, and sucrose are forms of sugar.**)

2. Conclude the lesson by discussing where an individual can get reliable information about nutrition. Some suggestions are the following: the family physician, home economics teachers, dieticians, nutrition centers, colleges and universities, publications of the USDA, the school nurse, and the National Dairy Council.

BACKGROUND INFORMATION

Traditionally, home economics teachers believed that if they presented factual nutrition information and diet plans that used the basic four food groups as a guide, students would make changes in their dietary habits. There is evidence to suggest this does not occur. It appears that knowledge alone does not usually influence a person to change health habits, especially regarding diet and exercise. A positive attitude and willingness to change must also be present.

A key step in nutrition education is for the student to gain nutrition knowledge and then use an evaluation tool to examine ideas and habits regarding nutrition.

The Daily Food Guide is the U.S. Government's adaptation of the basic four food groups. The new guide has added a fifth group, Fats-Sweets-Alcohol.

The Daily Food Guide has limitations on its use. Combination dishes are difficult to analyze, trace minderals may be consumed in inadequate quantities depending on food choices, and new fortified products do not easily fit into any of the food groups. However, the Daily Food Guide (basic four) is one of the easiest tools to use in selecting a balanced diet.

The tool used in these lessons is the Nutrient Analysis Method. In nutrient analysis, all of the food eaten by an individual within a given amount of time is recalled and analyzed. The use of a microcomputer and appropriate software is suggested for these lessons. If a microcomputer and software are not available, you may have to use the traditional hand calculation method of analysis.

To complete the analysis process, students list each food and the amount eaten in a 24-hour period on a "Dietary Recall" activity sheet. They note any special codes called for in the computer software. After this data is entered into the computer, a report is generated. The report is a compilation of the nutrients by percentage found in each food consumed. The student can then compare his or her profile with the Recommended Dietary Allowance (RDA). If a student were to track food consumption over a period of time, the results could be used to determine which nutrients are generally lacking, and point out which specific food habits need attention.

There are many nutrient analysis software programs available. They have their plusses and minuses. You should preview them carefully before making a selection to be sure the one you select meets your needs. Some examples of differences are the following: The Pennsylvania State University program only permits completing a one-day dietary recall analysis while others allow up to seven days of data collection. Several programs allow recipes to be added to the data base so individual ingredients do not have to be listed during a dietary analysis.

You may write to the companies to receive descriptions of the programs and their prices. Some of the programs available follow:

EATS
The Pennsylvania State University
Nutrition Education Center
University Park, PA 16802

EATING MACHINE
Muse Software
347 N. Charles Street
Baltimore, MD 21201

EAT SMART Nutrition Computer Program
The Pillsbury Company
M/S 3286
Pillsbury Center
Minneapolis, MN 55402

MENU CALC
Learning Seed
21250 N. Andover
Kildeer, IL 60047

EXTENSION ACTIVITIES

1. Ask each student to write a sample breakfast, lunch, dinner, and snack menu that fulfills the requirements for a well-balanced diet.
2. Invite a dietician to talk about the importance of nutrition in athletic training. How do those recommendations differ from someone not in training?

EAT SMART

You are now in one of the most critical growing periods of your life. Not since you were a toddler has your body grown as fast as it is now. You are undergoing more mental and physical changes than you will at any other time in your life. If this isn't enough, you also have to contend with the emotional stresses of adolescence!

Now is a time in your life when you must treat nutrition as a top priority. If you don't, you may pay a penalty in poor health the rest of your life. Do yourself a favor and vow you will not take nutritional shortcuts.

You and your friends all share some common goals. Among these are the desire to have plenty of energy, to be healthy and happy, and to be well-liked and attractive. Believe it! These things are possible for nearly every teenager. If you eat well-balanced meals each day, including foods from the basic four, include moderate exercise in your daily routine, and get sufficient rest and relaxation, you will be on top of the world!

Don't kid yourself about doing it later. The routine you establish now will stick with you for a lifetime. Now is when your body is growing, so NOW is when good living habits are most important. Your body is having enough trouble without you giving it a bunch of grief by not eating properly, by being a "couch potato," and by staying up all night.

Granted, you live a hectic life. But, a little planning will help you over the worst times. Some cardinal rules to follow: Avoid skipping meals or taking just a few bites on the run. Eat slowly. Did you know that if you do not adhere to these rules, you run the risk of overeating? If you eat slowly, your blood sugar level rises and your appetite is satisfied without a second helping.

It is important that you allow time for three meals a day. Skimping on one or two meals and then eating more at the remaining meal is not healthy. Such a procedure leads to weight and energy problems.

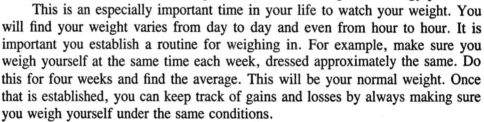

This is an especially important time in your life to watch your weight. You will find your weight varies from day to day and even from hour to hour. It is important you establish a routine for weighing in. For example, make sure you weigh yourself at the same time each week, dressed approximately the same. Do this for four weeks and find the average. This will be your normal weight. Once that is established, you can keep track of gains and losses by always making sure you weigh yourself under the same conditions.

You also need to know some other rules. If you are overweight, learn to take smaller helpings and to refuse seconds. Force yourself to eat slowly. Use less salt (or no salt) on your food. Salt causes your body to retain fluids, thus forcing your weight up. Too much salt is also related to heart disease.

Liquids are an important part of your dietary routine. At least four glasses of water per day in addition to milk and juices will be just fine. Don't skimp on the water. It is important because it contains important minerals needed by your body.

No one said growing up was easy! Do yourself a favor. Lay your personal foundation for good health and ideal weight by forming good eating and living habits. If you want to lead a long, healthy, happy, productive life—the time to start is NOW!

PERSONAL ENERGY ESTIMATE

In this activity, you will use a process to determine an estimate of how many calories your body needs daily to function properly. This process has five parts:

1. Determine your ideal body weight.
2. Determine the number of calories needed for basal metabolism.
3. Determine the number of calories needed for physical activity.
4. Determine the number of calories needed to digest food.
5. Determine the total number of calories needed by adding together the results from 2, 3, and 4.

You calculate your ideal body weight by completing the Frame Size and Age/Height/Weight sections below. Steps 2, 3, and 4 are determined by completing the appropriate section below. For example, to determine the number of calories needed for basal metabolism, complete the Calculating Basal Metabolism Calories section.

Step 1: Calculating Ideal Body Weight

FRAME SIZE

How tall are you? _____ feet _____ inches.

What is your frame size? To determine frame size, take your left hand and place the thumb and middle finger around your wrist.

    a. If your fingers overlap by more than one knuckle, you have a small frame.

    b. If your fingers overlap slightly, you have a medium frame.

    c. If your fingers do not meet or barely touch, you have a large frame.

Check the proper space to record your frame size:

_____ small   _____ medium   _____ large

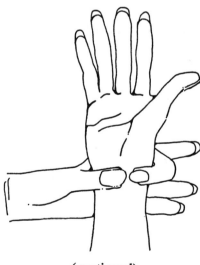

PERSONAL ENERGY ESTIMATE (continued)

AGE/HEIGHT/WEIGHT

On the chart below, circle your age and height:

	Age	Av. Ht.	Height Range	Av. Wt.	Weight Range
Boys	13	5'0"	57.3–63.7	95.6	77.4–133.8
	14	5'3"	59.6–66.4	107.9	87.8–128.0
	15	5'5"	62.5–68.7	121.7	101.1–142.3
Girls	13	5'0"	58.0–63.2	100.3	82.3–118.3
	14	5'2"	59.9–64.7	108.5	91.3–125.7
	15	5'3"	60.9–65.5	115.0	98.8–131.2

Based on the age/height/weight chart, your ideal weight is _____ lbs.

Compare your present weight with your ideal weight. Record the results:

_____ lbs. above ideal weight   _____ lbs. below ideal weight

For your height and frame size, you need to (check one):

_____ stay the same   _____ lose weight   _____ gain weight

Step 2: Calculating Basal Metabolism Calories

The reason there is a range of calories for a given height and age is that all people do not use the same number of calories for basal metabolism, do not participate in the same activities, and do not digest food to the same degree. To zero in on you personally, some mathematical calculations will have to be done.

First, locate your age on the Basal Metabolism Calories Chart and find the number of calories per square meter per hour for your sex. Multiply this figure by your body surface area in square meters and then multiply by 24 hours. See the Body Surface Area Chart.

(continued)

Name _____   Date _____

PERSONAL ENERGY ESTIMATE (continued)

BASAL METABOLISM CALORIES CHART
Calories Per Square Meter/Hour

Age	Males	Females
11	48.5	43.5
12	45.3	42.0
13	44.5	40.5
14	43.8	39.2
15	42.9	38.3
16	42.0	37.2
17	41.5	36.4

BODY SURFACE CHART

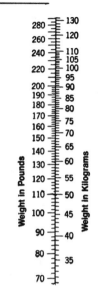

_____ × _____ = _____
Body Surface Area   Calories/Square Meter   Calories/Hour

_____ × 24 hours = _____
Calories/Hour   Basal Metab./Cal./Day

Step 3: Calculating Physical Activity Calories

    a. Determine your level of physical activity and enter the percentage here: _____
    20% = Sedentary   30% = Light   40% = Moderate   50% = Very Active
    b. Complete the following calculation:

_____ × _____ = _____
Basal Metabolism   Physical Activity   Physical Activity Cal.

(continued)

65

PERSONAL ENERGY ESTIMATE (continued)

Step 4: Calculating Food Digestion Calories

Your body uses energy in the form of calories to digest the food you eat. To determine the number of calories needed for this process, complete the following calculation:

_____ + _____ x 10% = _____
 Physical Activity Cal.   Basal Metabolic Cal.   Food Digestion Cal.

Step 5: Calculating Estimated Calories Needed Daily

To determine an estimate of the number of calories you need each day for your body to function properly, complete the following calculation:

_____ + _____ + _____ = _____
 Basal Metabolic Cal.   Physical Activity Cal.   Food Digestion Cal.   Total Daily Cal.
                                                                        Needed

NUTRIENT KNOWLEDGE

After you determine the number of calories you need, it is important to learn about nutrients and the role they play in good health.

There are six nutrient groups. Use the reference book provided by your teacher to complete the following chart:

Nutrient	Why it is Needed by the Body	Food Source
Protein		
Carbohydrate		
Fat		
B Vitamins		
Vitamin A		
Vitamin C		
Calcium and Phosphorus		
Iron		
Water		

Protein, carbohydrates, and fat are the energy-producing nutrients. According to the U.S. government, your diet should be made up of 12% protein, 30% fat, and 58% carbohydrate. Most of the fat (20%) should be unsaturated, and 48% of the carbohydrates should be complex, for example, vegetables and grains.

DIETARY RECALL

Now that you know the number of calories you need each day, you should learn whether your body is being nourished from the best food sources. Are you getting the right nutrients? That is the next step.

Write down everything you have eaten during the last 24 hours. Remember to list snacks. In some cases, you will need to consider the ingredients used to make the food. For example, if you ate a sandwich, list the bread, the filling, and what you used as the spread.

Food Eaten	Amount	Computer Code	No. of Servings

(Use the back of this sheet if you need more space to write.)

Breakfast

Lunch

Dinner

Snacks

Name _____ **Date** _____

DIET EVALUATION

1. Did your diet measure up? _____

2. What, if anything, do you need to eat less of? _____

   _____

   _____

3. What, if anything, do you need to add to your diet? _____

   _____

   _____

4. What percentage of your food intake came from:

   a. protein? _____ %

   b. carbohydrates? _____%

   c. fat? _____%

5. How does your percentage compare with the U.S. government's recommendations shown in the circle graph below?

   a. protein (+ or −) _____

   b. carbohydrates (+ or −) _____

   c. fat (+ or −) _____

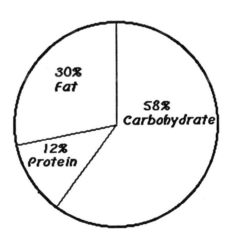

Name _____   Date _____

MENU PLAN

Your age: _____

Your energy needs? _____

BREAKFAST

_____

_____

_____

_____

LUNCH

_____

_____

_____

_____

DINNER

_____

_____

_____

_____

SNACKS

_____

_____

_____

_____

Estimated number of calories: _____
Number of servings from each of the basic four good groups:

  bread/cereal _____   milk/dairy _____

  vegetable/fruit _____   meat/poultry _____

HUMAN GROWTH AND DEVELOPMENT

■ CHILDREN AT PLAY

CONCEPTS

- Play affords opportunities for a child to develop physically, emotionally, socially, and mentally.
- Play activities are categorized as solitary, parallel, associative, or cooperative.

OBJECTIVES

The student will:

- recognize the value of play activities for young children
- identify the benefits of the different types of play activities
- describe and list examples of the four types of play activities

TEACHER PREPARATION

1. Make copies of the activity sheets "An Inventory," "Child's Play," "Types of Play," and "Play Observation Sheet."
2. Read the activity sheets for this lesson to determine the amount of background information you will need to complete the activities listed. Should you feel the need to brush up on your knowledge of the subject, some references you can use are *Caring for Children* by Mary Wanda Draper and Henry E. Draper (Peoria, IL: Charles A. Bennett Co.); *The Developing Child* by Holly E. Brisbane (Peoria, IL: Charles A. Bennett Co.); and *Teen Guide* by Valerie Chamberlain (New York: McGraw-Hill Book Company). These books have been published in many editions. You will find appropriate information in any edition, although some may be outdated.
3. Select a short children's story to be read aloud, collect puzzles, building blocks, pans to hold water, toys appropriate for water play, and balls for the activity "Child's Play."
4. Obtain pictures or posters of children engaging in solitary, parallel, associative, and cooperative play.
5. Arrange your teaching schedule to allow three class periods to complete these activities.
6. Organize your class into five small groups for the activity "Child's Play."

ACTIVITIES

Class Period 1

1. Begin this activity by asking students if they can remember some of the play activities they enjoyed most during their preschool days. Did they have a special friend or group of friends with whom they liked to play? Did they go to a day care center where there were organized activities? Did they play with toys or did they find other things to play with? Did they ever play alone? What role did their parents play in deciding what to do? Did they learn anything from these activities or were they just fun?

2. Explain that you are going to have them complete an inventory to see how much they already know about children's play. Distribute the activity sheet "An Inventory." When the students have finished completing the activity sheet, discuss the answers to the true-and-false questions in Part I. Briefly review the answers to Part II. It is important that students have an understanding of what makes up each of the four areas of growth and development. Conduct a discussion of the answers students gave in Part III. Make a list of these at the chalkboard or overhead projector. Separate the discussion/list into physical, emotional, social, and mental. You should add any important points students may have missed.

3. Conclude the discussion by emphasizing that play activities are an important part of growing up. What may look like just plain "play" may, in fact, be making an important contribution to the child's physical, emotional, social, or mental development.

Class Period 2

1. Distribute the activity sheet "Child's Play" and review the directions. The time students spend in each center is to be used to put the puzzle together, listen to the story, and so on. The purpose of this activity is to have students discover that play activities have a meaningful purpose beyond just having fun. Their purpose is to contribute to the emotional, physical, mental, and social development of the child. Through this activity, you are attempting to make this connection. Clarify any questions students may have. Assign students to one of the five groups you previously organized and have them go to their assigned center to begin working on the assignment. Allow groups to spend approximately five or six minutes at each center.

2. Conclude this activity with an open-ended discussion of the questions at the end of the activity sheet. Question five is especially important because it reinforces the notion that what may look like just plain ordinary fun is, in fact, playing an important part in the child's growth and development.

Class Period 3

It is important for students to know that play isn't just play. There are different kinds of play activities. Each of these contribute to the child's growth and development. The objective of this activity is to provide students with knowledge about four types of play activities and how they help children grow into well-rounded happy people. A straightforward lecture amply illustrated with visuals and concrete examples will give students the background they need to complete the activity sheet. Distribute the activity sheet ''Types of Play'' and begin. When you have completed presenting the basic content, ask students to give examples of each type they may have observed in younger brothers or sisters or at their day care center. Connect the concrete with the abstract here. Child growth and development should not be accidental. Responsible adults provide opportunities for all types of play activities. Ask them WHY.

PLAY INVENTORY

You are starting to learn about how children grow into healthy, happy adults. Part of this process involves play activities. How much do you know about children's play activities? Perhaps a lot more than you think you do! Let's check it out. If you don't know the answer, just try your best.

PART I: Read each statement. Place a T for true or an F for false in the space provided.

_____ 1. A child is aware that learning is taking place during play.

_____ 2. Education only takes place in school.

_____ 3. Play is work a child must do to grow.

_____ 4. The environment influences the way we grow and develop.

_____ 5. The essence of independence is to be able to do something for one's self.

_____ 6. Human growth and development occur in stages.

_____ 7. One stage of development has no relation to the next.

_____ 8. An adult's verbal interaction with a child is important to the development of a positive self-image.

_____ 9. A person with a positive self-concept feels good about himself or herself.

_____ 10. A person with a positive self-concept is usually timid around others.

_____ 11. There are different types of play activities.

_____ 12. Solitary play activities are bad for the child.

_____ 13. Children learn many things from their play experiences.

_____ 14. Adult supervision of play activities is not necessary since children grow and develop in stages naturally.

_____ 15. Playing tag is an example of a mental activity.

(continued)

PLAY INVENTORY (continued)

PART II: Play activities provide children with opportunities to grow physically, socially, emotionally, and mentally. Read the statements below and place a P for physical, S for social, E for emotional, or M for mental in the space provided to describe the activity listed.

_____ 1. Riding a tricycle

_____ 2. Listening to a story

_____ 3. Hitting a peg with a hammer

_____ 4. Having a tea party

_____ 5. Playing "Pin the Tail on the Donkey"

_____ 6. Putting a puzzle together

_____ 7. Jumping rope

_____ 8. Being afraid of lightning and thunder

_____ 9. Listening to music

_____ 10. Learning how to play a game

_____ 11. Playing house

_____ 12. Going to the movies with a friend

PART III: Make a list of the ways play activities help children to grow and develop. Try to include all four areas of a child's development: social, physical, emotional, and mental.

SOCIAL: _____

_____

PHYSICAL: _____

_____

EMOTIONAL: _____

_____

MENTAL: _____

_____

CHILD'S PLAY

Just for fun, we are going to play today! Pretend you are a preschool child. You and a group of friends are going to participate in five play activities. These are: building blocks, a water table, stories, puzzles, and bouncing balls. You are to go to each of the five centers and pretend you are a small child participating in the play activity contained in the center. Your group will spend five or six minutes in each center. Try to think about what you are learning at each center. Have fun!

Now that you have had a chance to practice being a kid again, it's time to think about how play activities, such as these, contribute to the growth and development of a child. Write your answers to the following questions in the spaces provided.

(continued)

CHILD'S PLAY (continued)

1. Name the type of activity represented in each play center:

   a. building blocks _____

   b. water table _____

   c. stories _____

   d. puzzles _____

   e. balls _____

   Remember, it is possible that a center could provide more than one type of activity!

2. Pick one of the centers and briefly describe what a child might learn by participating in the activity.

   _____

   _____

   _____

3. Based upon your experience, how would you define play?

   _____

   _____

   _____

4. Did all of the centers fit your description? If not, which didn't? _____

   _____ How do you explain that? _____

   _____

5. Compare your experiences at school with your experiences at the five play centers. How were they

   similar? _____

   _____

   How were they different? _____

   _____

TYPES OF PLAY ACTIVITIES

There are different types of play activities. One method of describing them is to call them "active" or "passive." Active ones are those in which the child is actually doing something; for example, playing the game. Passive ones are those in which the child is an observer; for example, watching the game. It is important to recognize that children need both of these kinds of play. There are several other "types" of play activities that children should experience also. Your teacher will be discussing the different types of play activities and how they help young children develop. Listen carefully and answer the following questions.

1. How does a child get satisfaction from active play? _____

_____

_____

2. What does a child do in active play? _____

_____

3. How does a child get satisfaction from passive play? _____

_____

_____

4. What are some forms of passive play? _____

_____

5. Describe solitary play and give an example. _____

_____

_____

_____

_____

© 1990 by The Center for Applied Research in Education

(continued)

TYPES OF PLAY ACTIVITIES (continued)

6. Describe parallel play and give an example.

_____

_____

_____

_____

7. Describe associative play and give an example. _____

_____

_____

_____

_____

8. Describe cooperative play and give an example. _____

_____

_____

_____

_____

9. Younger children are more likely to participate in _____

   and _____ play.

10. Older children spend more time engaging in _____

   and _____ play activities.

11. List several tips on how to keep play activities a positive experience. Use the back of this sheet if you need more space to write. _____

_____

_____

■ A CHILD'S LEARNING TOOLS

CONCEPTS

- Appropriate toys encourage a child to develop motor, mental, and social skills.
- Playing with appropriate toys can provide an emotional outlet for a child.
- To be suitable, play materials should be related to the child's level of physical, mental, emotional, and social development.

OBJECTIVES

The student will:

- learn the criteria to use in selecting children's toys
- learn what type of children's toys are appropriate for different stages of a child's development
- be able to identify types of play activities through systematic observation
- learn to evaluate the suitability of toys through systematic observation of children at play

TEACHER PREPARATION

1. Make copies of the activity sheets "Toy Selection," "Toys for a Purpose," "Toys for Different Ages," "How Old Am I?" and "Observations."
2. After studying the activity sheets, should you feel the need for additional information, check the resources suggested in the previous lesson.
3. Collect a selection of toys appropriate for each age group listed in the activity sheet "Toys for Different Ages." This collection should include examples for each of the categories listed on the activity sheets "Toy Selection" and "Toys for Different Types of Play." Arrange them in a display where they are easily visible and accessible to the students.
4. Make arrangements with a day care center, nursery school, or kindergarten class for your students to observe children playing with various types of toys.
5. Complete your usual field-trip procedure of parental permission slips, transportation, and so on.
6. Arrange your schedule to allow four class periods for the activities outlined below.
7. Note that two options are given for Class Period 1. Choose one of these.
8. Prepare a file of pictures or posters showing children of different ages in a variety of play activities.

Your school librarian may be able to help you with this. Many libraries will have a vertical file entitled "Play."

ACTIVITIES

Class Period 1

1. Open this lesson by making the statement, "Toys are a child's tools." Ask students what they think this old saying means. Do adults choose tools that are appropriate for the job they want to do? Is it possible that a child's "tools" should be selected in a similar way? The answer is obvious. Distribute the activity sheet "Toy Selection." Direct the students to read the introductory information and complete the activity sheet. The directions for completing the activity sheet will depend upon which of the two given options you choose. Option 1 is a straightforward lecture/ discussion about the purpose of toys and toy construction, safety, appearance, design, and cost. Have the students complete the activity sheet as you conduct your lecture/discussion. To conclude this activity, hold up a sample toy that is safe, for example. Have the students identify the features that make it safe. Do the same thing for each of the other categories. Option 2 suggests you distribute resource material about toy selection that students are to read and complete the activity sheet. Conclude the activity in the manner described above.

2. In this part of the lesson, you will be teaching students how types of play activities and types of toys are related. Begin by describing different types of play activities: (1) active physical play; (2) manipulative, constructive, creative play; (3) imitative, imaginative, dramatic play; and (4) social play. Illustrate these with pictures and posters. Point out the different types of toys that are being used in the different situations. Ask students what conclusion they can draw from your discussion and the pictures you have shown them. (The type of play activity should dictate the type of toys with which children are provided.) Distribute the activity sheet "Toys for a Purpose." Have the students read the introductory information, answer any questions they may have, and help them start completing the activity sheet. When they have finished this task, give the students an example of a play activity and have them select an appropriate toy from the collection. Take this opportunity to make sure they know *why* it is appropriate.

Class Period 2

1. Ask students how they can tell the age group for which a toy is intended. Have some examples of packaging to circulate for the students to see. Why do toy manufacturers do this? If a toy does not contain this kind of information, what are the risks to the consumer? Distribute the activity sheet "Toys for Different Ages." Have the students read about the characteristics of one- to six-year-olds in the child development section of their textbook. After students have finished their reading, ask the students to suggest guidelines for selecting toys for a child from infancy to the age of two years. Write the guidelines on the chalkboard or overhead projector. Continue using this technique until a set of guidelines is completed for each of the age groups listed. Have the students examine the toys you collected for class. Ask them to identify toys appropriate for each age group and describe why it is appropriate.

2. Distribute the activity sheet "How Old Am I?" and have the students complete it. Briefly review students' responses. You may want to have a volunteer read "Remember the right toy . . ."

3. Explain the details of the field trip the class will be taking during the next class period. Be sure to review how students are to use "Observations." The key to worthwhile observation is that it must be *systematic*. If it is not systematic, the observer may see a lot of things that mean nothing.

Class Period 3

Check any last-minute "housekeeping chores" related to the field trip. Briefly review what students will be observing. Remind students they are guests in a learning environment. It is important they be as unobtrusive as possible. During your stay in the day care center or kindergarten, help students with their observations. Comment upon the selection of toys available, their appropriateness for the age level of the children and the type of play activities being carried out, and so on. If you make the trip to the center by bus, use the time of the return trip to let students react to the experience. Before students leave the bus, review what their task will be during the next class period. They should organize their notes so that they will be able to discuss their systematic observation accordingly.

Class Period 4

Begin today's class with a discussion of the characteristics of the age group of children the students observed during the prior class period. Make a list of these at the chalkboard or overhead projector. Move on to a discussion of the students' observations for each of the scenarios listed. Conclude the lesson by asking students if the play activities and materials (toys) being used were appropriate for the children in attendance. Have them explain why or why not. Should you want to give a short quiz on this lesson, such questions as the following could be asked.

a. List three reasons play is a valuable experience for young children.

b. Describe an activity for preschoolers that uses large muscles.

c. Describe an activity that requires eye-hand coordination.

d. Describe a play activity that promotes social development.

e. Describe a play activity that promotes emotional development.

f. Describe an activity that would be considered solitary play.

g. Describe a cooperative play activity for a four- to six-year-old.

TOY SELECTION

Toys are one of the tangible things that touch children's lives. The use of toys in play activities helps children try out new concepts, find out more about reality, and learn to communicate with the world around them. Sometimes adults forget about or fail to understand the importance of toys to a child's development. They see toys as a distraction rather than tools that contribute to the child's social, emotional, physical, and mental growth.

Because toys play such an important part in most children's play activities, it is important to know how to select toys that are appropriate. Your teacher will provide you with reference information about the important points to consider when purchasing toys. Study this material and make a list of these points in each of the categories below:

SAFETY _____

_____

CONSTRUCTION _____

_____

PURPOSE _____

_____

APPEARANCE _____

_____

DESIGN _____

_____

COST _____

_____

85

TOYS FOR A PURPOSE

Children have many different play interests. They enjoy active physical play. They enjoy quiet activities. They enjoy imitating the activities of adults. They add their own creative touches to these activities. They enjoy taking things apart and putting them back together. They touch them, taste them, look at them, and turn them, as they try to find out how they are made and what they can do with them. As children grow older, their interests broaden to include sounds, words, numbers, time, space, and distance. In adult language, they develop interest in "subjects"—art, music, science, nature, and literature. These interests are evident in the type of toys and other things they use in their play activities.

It is important to provide children with toys that satisfy their interest in physical play; manipulative, constructive, creative play; imitative, imaginative, dramatic play; and social play. Use the reference information provided by your teacher to list the type of toys most appropriate for the activities listed below:

ACTIVE PHYSICAL PLAY _____

_____

_____

MANIPULATIVE, CONSTRUCTIVE, CREATIVE PLAY _____

_____

_____

IMITATIVE, IMAGINATIVE, DRAMATIC PLAY _____

_____

_____

SOCIAL PLAY _____

_____

_____

Name _____   Date _____

TOYS FOR DIFFERENT AGES

There is another important factor to take into consideration when selecting a toy. Is it suitable for the age of the child who will be playing with it? Generally, toys are divided into age groups: infancy to two years; two to four years (nursery school age); and four to six years (kindergarten age). There are age groupings for older children, but our focus is on young children.

Consult your reference material and notes from class discussions. In the space provided, describe the types of toys that best meet the needs of children in the age groupings given below.

  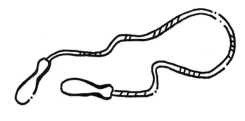

INFANCY TO TWO YEARS _____

_____

_____

_____

TWO TO FOUR YEARS _____

_____

_____

_____

FOUR TO SIX YEARS _____

_____

_____

_____

_____

Name _____   Date _____

HOW OLD AM I?

We have discussed a lot of things about children's play activities and toys. Let's take time out and check to see how much you remember. Read the descriptions below and answer the questions in the spaces provided.

1. I have a lot of curiosity and a high degree of imagination. I am interested in learning how to write and tell time. I enjoy being with other children and playing group games.

   a. How old am I? _____

   b. What toys are appropriate for me? _____

   _____

   c. Why are they appropriate? _____

   _____

2. I enjoy sights and sounds. I just learned how to pick up objects. I touch them, taste them, and hit other objects with them.

   a. How old am I? _____

   b. What toys are appropriate for me? _____

   _____

   c. Why are they appropriate? _____

   _____

3. I am very active physically and have a vivid imagination. I like to talk, ride my tricycle, and explore things and places. I like to imitate grownups.

   a. How old am I? _____

   b. What toys are appropriate for me? _____

   _____

   c. Why are they appropriate? _____

   _____

Name _____   Date _____

OBSERVATIONS

This may be your first time to observe children in a group setting. It is easy to get distracted because there is so much going on. You will get more information from your observation if you use a system. For example, your task today is to observe five types of play activities. Study the questions below so that you are thoroughly familiar with the types of activities you are looking for. Start with the first one. Take a quick look around the room to find an example. If you don't see an example, go on to the next type. Continue this process until you have all five examples. When you have finished, make a list of things that are happening that you want to ask a question about. Why did the kids do this or that? Why did the teacher give the child that particular toy? And so on. Have a good visit!

1. Describe a situation involving social interaction between two or more children.

_____

_____

_____

_____

2. Describe an activity that promoted creative expression.

_____

_____

_____

_____

3. Describe a toy that promoted large muscle development through a physical play activity.

_____

_____

_____

_____

4. Describe an activity that promoted mental growth.

_____

_____

_____

_____

5. Describe a situation in which a child expressed a feeling or became emotional.

_____

_____

_____

_____

OBSERVATIONS (continued)

6. Questions I want to ask:

_____

_____

_____

_____

_____

_____

_____

_____

_____

_____

_____

_____

_____

_____

_____

_____

_____

_____

_____

_____

_____

_____

_____

_____

_____

■ TOY SAFETY

CONCEPTS

- Safety is an important consideration in the selection of children's toys.
- Children's toys should be hazard free.

OBJECTIVES

The student will:

- learn the characteristics of safe toys
- evaluate toys for level of safety
- develop a set of safety guidelines to use in toy selection

TEACHER PREPARATION

1. Make copies of the activity sheets "What Do You Know About Toy Safety?", "Toy Evaluation," and "Safety Guidelines for Toy Selection."
2. Review your knowledge of toy safety, if necessary. You can do a quick review by looking at the activity sheet "What Do You Know About Toy Safety?"
3. The United States Consumer Product Safety Commission (Washington, D.C. 20207) publishes several pamphlets about toy safety. Some examples are *For Kids' Sake Think Toy Safety* and *Toy Safety Always in Season. Selecting Toys: The Choice Is Yours* by Joyce Nies Richardson is available from the Vocational Agriculture Service, College of Agriculture, University of Illinois, 434 Munford Hall, Urbana, IL 61801. *How to Choose Toys* by Grace Langdon is available from the Toy Institute, Inc., 1107 Broadway, New York, NY 10010. Order enough copies to distribute to your class. Allow four to six weeks for delivery.
4. You will need a collection of toys that contains both safe and unsafe examples. Have at least one toy per class member. Arrange the toys in an attractive, easily visible display.
5. Divide the class into three groups for the activity to be completed in Class Period 3. Group 1 will develop guidelines for infancy to two years, Group 2 for two- to four-year-olds, and Group 3 for four- to six-year-olds.

ACTIVITIES

Class Period 1

1. Begin this lesson by reviewing what students have learned about toys to date, especially that they should be selected with a particular age group and purpose in mind. Point out that there is another very important consideration—safety. Unfortunately, not all toys are as safe as they should be even though we have governmental oversight. Unscrupulous manufacturers and importers still market cheap, dangerous toys. Distribute the activity sheet "What Do You Know About Toy Safety?" along with reference works about toy safety, pamphlets from the Product Safety Commission, and so on. Explain to the students that they may already know a lot about toy safety. They should try to answer the questions without using any reference material. If they are unsure or do not know the answer, they should look it up.

2. When the students have completed the activity sheet, begin to discuss each question. Clear up any misconceptions the students may have. Show examples for questions 3, 4, 5, and 6. You should include both safe and unsafe examples, if possible.

3. Explain to the students that in the next class, they will be evaluating toys. They will not only be checking for safety, but will also be making an evaluation of their appropriateness for the age level indicated.

Class Period 2

1. Briefly review the list of toy safety features that were discussed in the last lesson. Also review how toys should be appropriate for both age level and their intended purpose.

2. Distribute the activity sheet "Toy Evaluation" and review the directions for completing it. If you have any special directions about how students are to select the toys for evaluation, review them also. Be prepared for more than the usual classroom noise level, especially if you have any musical toys to be evaluated. Assist students as they complete their evaluation.

3. When students have completed the evaluation, have class members share their conclusions with the class. Always ask *why*. Have the students point out or demonstrate why the toy is safe or unsafe. Why would they or would they not select the toy? Why is it appropriate or not for the age level indicated? What type of play activities could it be used for?

4. Alert the class that during the next lesson, they will be developing a set of guidelines to be used to select toys for the various age groups. They should review their notes from all of the lessons completed to date so that they will be able to complete the assignment with ease.

Class Period 3

1. Distribute the activity sheet "Draft Guidelines for Toy Selection." Review the scenario and the directions. Assign students to their groups, answer any questions, and let the students get to work. Allow the students to use their notes and any reference material to complete the activity.

2. When the students have completed this task, conduct a discussion of what they have listed. Make

a list of these at the chalkboard or overhead projector for each age group. When finished, have the class choose toys that should be included on the "Recommended Toy Selection Guidelines" list and have the students write them on their activity sheet. This activity will synthesize the toy selection information students learned in the last three lessons.

Name _____   Date _____

WHAT DO YOU KNOW ABOUT TOY SAFETY?

You have probably played with a lot of toys in your lifetime! It could be that you are already an expert on toy safety. Study each statement below and mark if it is true or false. Then comes the hard part! Give the reason why you marked the statement as you did. If you are unsure or simply do not have any idea of the correct response, use the reference materials your teacher has provided to find the answer.

T   F   1. People with common sense have little to learn about toy safety.

Why? _____

_____

_____

T   F   2. Few children are hurt each year using toys.

Why? _____

_____

_____

T   F   3. Stuffed toys are soft and cuddly, never dangerous.

Why? _____

_____

_____

T   F   4. The worst thing to be said about toys that break easily is that they are a waste of money.

Why? _____

_____

_____

T   F   5. Consumers should look for labels on all toys they purchase.

Why? _____

_____

_____

T   F   6. Toys can be too advanced for a child.

Why? _____

_____

_____

T   F   7. The most important function of a toy box is to teach children to be neat and orderly.

Why? _____

_____

_____

(continued)

WHAT DO YOU KNOW ABOUT TOY SAFETY? (continued)

T F   8. Children should be encouraged to use toys in any way they wish so their creativity and imagination grow.

Why? _____

_____

_____

T F   9. Children need constant supervision when they play.

Why? _____

_____

_____

T F   10. The government bans toys that are not safe.

Why? _____

_____

_____

T F   11. Toys not banned by the government are safe for children of any age.

Why? _____

_____

_____

T F   12. Broken toys should be repaired under the supervision of an adult.

Why? _____

_____

_____

Name _____   Date _____

TOY EVALUATION

Select a toy from those displayed in your classroom. Look it over closely. Try to figure out the age level and type of play activity for which it is most appropriate. Then complete the questions below.

Name of toy and/or description: _____
_____

1. Is the toy labeled to indicate the appropriate age level?

_____ If not, what age level do you think is appropriate?

_____ Why?

_____
_____

2. What materials are used in the toy's construction? _____

_____
_____

3. Does the toy have sharp points that could puncture a child? _____ If yes, describe: _____

_____

4. Does the toy have sharp edges that could cut a child's skin? _____ If yes, describe: _____

_____

5. If the toy is made of plastic, is it durable enough to survive rough play? _____ How do you

know? _____

_____

6. Are there small parts that could be swallowed or inhaled? _____ If yes, describe: _____

_____

© 1990 by The Center for Applied Research in Education

(continued)

TOY EVALUATION (continued)

7. Does the toy involve shooting or throwing objects? _____ If yes, what are they? _____
_____

Are they safe? _____ Why? _____
_____

8. Does the toy make loud, piercing noises? _____ If yes, describe the safety hazard: _____
_____

9. Is the color of the toy pleasing to the eye? _____

10. Is the surface easily cleaned? _____

11. Is the toy noninflammable? _____

12. Will the toy withstand weather and/or hard use? _____

13. Can the toy be used for more than one type of play activity? _____ If yes, list some: _____
_____

14. Does the toy stimulate:

   a. curiosity? _____　　e. problem solving? _____

   b. interest? _____　　f. imagination? _____

   c. manipulation? _____　　g. creativity? _____

   d. initiative? _____

15. Does the toy promote growth toward:

   a. independence? _____　　c. group activity? _____

   b. exploration? _____　　d. social relationships? _____

16. Overall, this toy is: safe _____ unsafe _____

Why? _____
_____
_____
_____

DRAFT GUIDELINES FOR TOY SELECTION

Our class has been asked by a local day care center for advice about selecting toys for children in the infancy to two-year, two- to four-year, and four- to six-year-old age ranges. Each of us must do our part if we are to come up with the best possible list of suggestions.

Your teacher will assign you one of the age groups. Your job is to develop a set of safety and child development principle guidelines to use to select toys for your age group. You may use your notes from the previous lessons and any reference materials available in our classroom.

You will notice the title to this activity uses the word "draft." That was done for a reason. After we develop our individual lists, we will combine all of our lists into a final set of criteria. As the old saying goes, many heads are better than one!

AGE GROUP: _____

GUIDELINES: _____

_____

_____

_____

_____

_____

_____

_____

_____

_____

_____

_____

_____

_____

_____

_____

_____

_____

Name _____   Date _____

RECOMMENDED TOY SELECTION GUIDELINES

After the class has agreed upon the guidelines to recommend to the day care center, write them in the spaces below.

INFANCY TO TWO YEARS

_____

_____

_____

_____

_____

TWO YEARS TO FOUR YEARS

_____

_____

_____

_____

_____

FOUR YEARS TO SIX YEARS

_____

_____

_____

_____

_____

■ STORYTELLING

CONCEPTS

- Storytelling is an ancient art.
- Storytelling can encourage a child to want to read.
- Storytelling helps young children learn.

OBJECTIVES

The student will:

- listen to a story being read by the teacher
- evaluate storybooks according to selected criteria
- practice reading a story
- read a story to a group of three or four preschool children

TEACHER PREPARATION

1. Select several examples of storybooks to discuss, read, and evaluate. Examples should include both appropriate and inappropriate stories for the age level being considered so that comparisons can be made.
2. Prepare copies of the activity sheets "Story Telling," "Evaluation of a Children's Book," "Storytelling Tips," "Storytelling Evaluation Checklist," and "Self-Evaluation."

ACTIVITIES

Class Period 1

1. Motivate interest in the storytelling activity by discussing the following information. Storytelling is an art almost as ancient as the human race. Stories were told about the sun, moon, stars, and events affecting the tribe or village. Early stories were combined with songs and dances. They were passed on from one family member to another, mostly by word of mouth until the invention of the printing press in the 1400's.

2. Show students several books that have examples of colorful animated figures, different size illustrations, and appropriate vocabulary for the target age level. Include educational storybooks and books that have action. They should not be too complicated. Point out that most children like stories that rhyme.

3. Show students several books that are not appropriate for the students being considered. Ask the students to identify what is wrong with them.

4. Distribute the activity sheet ''Storytelling'' and review the information. Read a story to the class, such as *The Cat in the Hat* by Dr. Seuss. Allow students to interact with you while you read the story. Have students observe your reading style.

5. Distribute storybooks and the activity sheet ''Evaluation of a Children's Book.'' Have students complete the activity sheet. Review the information about storytelling. Allow time for students to talk about the book they evaluated.

Class Period 2

1. Review the information on ''Storytelling Tips.'' Explain to the students that they are going to prepare to read a story to a group of three or four young children.

2. Have students select a story to read. They should practice reading it several times and then read it to a classmate. They should have a classmate complete the ''Storytelling Evaluation Checklist.'' If you do not have enough class time for this activity, have students read into a tape recorder or in front of a mirror, and complete the checklist as a self-evaluation.

3. Schedule time for students to read their stories to a kindergarten class, nursery school, day care center, or Sunday school class. If this is not possible, consider inviting children to class. Students could also check with the community library and volunteer to read a story at one of the library's story hours.

4. Have students plan a follow-up activity to leave with the children. Follow-up activities can include pictures to color, simple one-word crossword puzzles, a two- or three-piece puzzle, or worksheets with matching sections (such as a picture to a word), and so on.

5. After all students have had the opportunity to read a story to their audience, have them discuss how it went. What would they do the same? What would they do differently? How did they feel when they were reading the story? What behaviors did the youngsters exhibit? Why? Have the students complete ''Self-Evaluation.''

Name _____   Date _____

STORYTELLING

You have learned how to select an appropriate storybook. Listed below are some techniques to use to help you become a terrific storyteller. Study them carefully.

1. PURPOSES OF STORYTELLING
    a. to have fun
    b. to teach the child information
    c. to encourage the child to want to learn to read
2. THINGS TO CONSIDER IN SELECTING A BOOK OR STORY
    a. age and composition of the group
    b. storyteller's likes and dislikes
    c. reason for telling the story (bedtime, playtime)
3. REQUIREMENTS FOR A POSITIVE STORYTELLING EXPERIENCE
    a. storyteller must enjoy telling/reading the story
    b. voice and diction should have these characteristics (practice with a tape recorder)
        (1) good intonation
        (2) proper volume
        (3) clarity
        (4) expression
    c. your appearance should have these traits
        (1) sitting or standing in a
            relaxed position
        (2) free of large dangling jewelry,
            gaudy dress, and extreme hairstyles

Name _____   Date _____

EVALUATION OF A CHILDREN'S BOOK

Your task today is to evaluate a storybook. Complete the identification information about the book you are going to evaluate, and then proceed to the evaluation section.

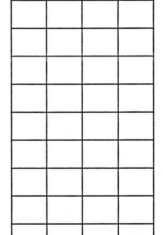

TITLE: _____

_____

AUTHOR: _____

ILLUSTRATOR: _____

PUBLISHER: _____

DATE OF PUBLICATION: _____
- -

Rate the book by placing an X in the box that best describes your evaluation. The rating scale is:

3 = Excellent   2 = Good   1 = Poor   NA = Not Applicable

THIS BOOK:

	3	2	1	NA
1. has colorful illustrations				
2. uses appropriate speech patterns				
3. has appropriate vocabulary for age group				
4. eliminates sex-role stereotyping				
5. helps children use their imagination				
6. shows appropriate behavior				
7. motivates children to learn				
8. follows a logical sequence of events				
9. has illustrations that fit the script				
10. promotes understanding others				

(continued)

EVALUATION OF A CHILDREN'S BOOK (continued)

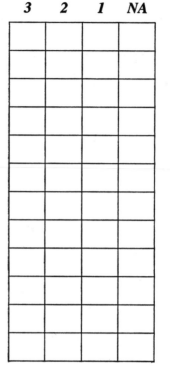

	3	2	1	NA
11. promotes an appreciation of animals				
12. helps children deal with their feelings				
13. is made with sturdy paper				
14. is well bound				
15. has a sturdy cover				
16. is easy to handle				
17. has appropriate-size type				
18. has an appropriate theme				
19. is free of prejudice				
20. portrays people of various races				
21. has a lot of action				
22. appeals to at least one of the senses				

SUMMARY:

1. How long would it take to read this book? _____

2. What would children most enjoy about this book? _____

_____

_____

3. How could this book be improved? _____

_____

_____

4. Would you purchase this book for a three- or four-year-old? _____

   Why? _____

_____

_____

STORYTELLING TIPS

Study the information below. It will help you prepare for your storytelling experience.

1. PRACTICE TECHNIQUES
   a. Read the story carefully, visualize the characters and scenes, and think of ways to make it "come alive."
   b. Practice reading the story aloud, making note of special vocabulary, unusual phrases, or rhythm.
   c. Pay special attention to practicing any dialogue.
   d. Practice in front of a mirror or with a tape recorder.
   e. Prepare key questions about your story.

2. PRESENTATION TECHNIQUES/PROCEDURES
   a. Sit the children on the floor directly in front of you where all can see the illustrations.
   b. Introduce the book by telling children the title, author, subject of the story, special information about the author, and so on. Your introduction needs to get the children's attention.

   c. Maintain eye contact. This gives the child the feeling that the story is being told especially for him or her. Be familiar enough with the story that you do not need to keep your eyes on the page at all times.
   d. Use facial expressions, especially of your eyes, smiles, frowns, and so on. Practice your expressions in front of a mirror.
   e. Show children the illustrations. Do not be in a hurry about this. Give them plenty of time to see them.
   f. Hold the book to one side while reading. Tilt the book downward when showing illustrations.
   g. Be aware that children will probably make some remarks while you are reading the story. Decide if you want to hold discussions during the story, acknowledge questions with a nod of your head, or saying something like "You can tell us about that at the end of the story." You will have to use your own judgment about this when it occurs. For example, you might want to help children see significant ideas, events, or characters by answering questions or pointing out details in the text and illustrations.
   h. Prepare a reply for the statement "I've already heard about that!"
   i. Prepare your concluding remarks.

Name _____   Date _____

STORYTELLING EVALUATION CHECKLIST

Now that you are going to be reading a story to a group of young children, it is time to do some practicing and have someone else check how you are doing. Have a classmate listen to you read the story. Ask the classmate to look at the descriptors below and place a checkmark in the appropriate column to indicate his or her impressions.

	Needs Improvement	Satisfactory	Good
1. General Attitude			
a. visible enjoyment of the story			
b. relaxed			
2. Appearance			
a. no distracting mannerisms			
b. good posture			
c. varied facial expressions			
3. Voice and Diction			
a. volume			
b. clarity			
c. intonation			
d. expression			
4. Presentation			
a. familiarity with the story			
b. eye contact			
c. position of book			
d. shows illustrations slowly			
e. introduction			
f. conclusion			

SELF-EVALUATION

Now that you have had some experience telling a story, it is time to take a few minutes to check on how well you think things went. Look at the descriptors below and place a checkmark in the appropriate column to indicate your impressions.

1 = NEEDS MORE WORK   2 = SATISFACTORY   3 = GOOD

	1	2	3
1. I chose a book appropriate for three- and four-year-olds.			
2. I introduced the story before beginning to read.			
3. I was familiar with the story.			
4. I had good eye contact with the audience.			
5. I held the book so that the audience could easily see the illustrations.			
6. I involved the audience with the story.			
7. I had a summary or a conclusion.			
8. I took 10 to 15 minutes for the storytelling.			

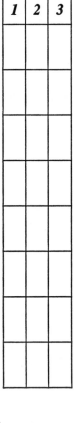

■ FOODS FOR CHILDREN

CONCEPTS

- Meal time should be a pleasant experience.
- Eating habits and attitudes formed in childhood may remain throughout life.

OBJECTIVES

The student will:

- learn about the importance of the physical and emotional environment at mealtime
- learn about the importance of appetite appeal in meal planning
- learn about proper feeding and eating utensils

TEACHER PREPARATION

1. Read the suggested Background Information regarding the physical and emotional environment, size of portion, and nutrition requirements for preschool children.
2. Obtain several examples of bottles; training drinking cups; strained, instant, and creamed baby foods; child-sized flatware and plates; and cereal.
3. Prepare copies of the activity sheets "Foods for Children" and "A Nutritious Snack."

ACTIVITIES

1. Ask the students if they can remember if they had any favorite foods when they were a small child. Did they have a high chair? A special place at the table? Their own dish that may have had a storybook character painted on it? Children's eating experiences should be made as pleasant as possible. Mealtime should be a happy time.
2. Distribute the activity sheet "Foods for Children." Have students complete the activity sheet as you present information about feeding children. Allow for interaction among class members. While discussing the feeding of infants, show the bottles, cereal, different types of foods, and the proper spoon to use in feeding. List the order in which foods are introduced into the diet of an infant (breast milk or formula, cereals, fruits and vegetables, meats, finger foods).

3. Distribute and have students complete the activity sheet ''A Nutritious Snack.'' When they have completed their menu, take a few minutes to discuss their ideas. From their suggestions, decide on several snack menus that could be used during the playschool activity. (See the lesson titled ''Playschool.'') This list can be used by the group of students whose job it will be to plan the snack center for the playschool.

BACKGROUND INFORMATION

In your discussion, you should explain to the students that small children react to how food looks, tastes, and feels just as they do. Food should have variety in its color, flavor, and texture. Variety in texture can be achieved by serving something soft, something chewy, and something crunchy. Children have sensitive taste buds. Therefore, foods should have mild, delicate flavor. Variety in color can be achieved by serving vegetables or fruits with different colors. For example, serve carrots and green beans with chicken. You can also add variety by cutting foods into different shapes and by having varied temperatures.

The environment where a child eats should be bright, well-ventilated, and clean. A child should be seated in a high chair or some other form of chair so that his or her feet will rest on something firm. Plates, cups, and eating utensils should be sized so that they can be managed by small hands.

Mealtime should be a happy time. Eating is fun for the hungry child. A tired, excited child cannot enjoy food. Help the child to calm down and come to the table relaxed and clean. Serve attractive food, small servings, and allow some freedom to choose his or her own food and eat his or her own way. Conversation at the table should be interesting and peaceful. Accept occasional table accidents as a normal part of growing up.

Some children have stronger feelings about how and what they eat than others. Each child needs an opportunity to become acquainted with a variety of foods. As the child gets older, he or she likes to make choices. If the child is not fond of vegetables, offer a choice between two vegetables. The foods a child chooses or refuses are likely to reflect the attitudes of someone else he or she knows. Try serving different foods when the child is hungry. Invite the child's friends for a meal if you know the friend eats the food you are trying to encourage your child to eat. Decorate the food so it has appetite appeal.

FOODS FOR CHILDREN

When babies are born, they need love, care, a good emotional environment, and nutritious food. In this lesson, we are going to be focusing on children's food needs. We will also be talking about other aspects of feeding—the utensils we use, the proper environment, and so on. There is more to feeding the baby than just picking the right foods! Habits and attitudes are important because those formed in our early years often remain with us for the rest of our life.

Your teacher will be presenting a lot of information about foods for children. Listen closely and answer the questions below. It is important your information is correct because you will use it to plan a real menu for the playschool we will have later.

1. What kind of food does a baby need when it is born? _____

_____ or _____

2. A child is introduced to the following foods as it grows older:

_____

_____

_____

_____

_____

3. Food's appearance, taste, and texture are important to the development of good eating attitudes. How can you provide variety in color, flavor, and texture?

_____

_____

_____

_____

_____

_____

_____

(continued)

FOODS FOR CHILDREN (continued)

4. A good physical environment at mealtime is important. How can we provide for these environmental needs?

_____

_____

_____

_____

_____

_____

5. What can we do to make mealtime a happy time?

_____

_____

_____

_____

_____

_____

_____

6. Some children have strong feelings about what and how they eat. What can we do to direct a child's reaction to food?

_____

_____

_____

_____

_____

_____

_____

_____

_____

A NUTRITIOUS SNACK

Plan three nutritious snacks for three- or four-year-olds. The class will consider your suggestions for our playschool snack menu.

MENU 1

_____

_____

_____

_____

_____

MENU 2

_____

_____

_____

_____

_____

MENU 3

_____

_____

_____

_____

_____

_____

■ PLAYSCHOOL

CONCEPTS

- Structured activities and time spent with young children help to develop positive communication and interaction skills in youth and young adults.
- Opportunities to apply knowledge of child growth and development is an important part of a young person's education.
- Students learn important skills by selecting, setting up, and implementing a series of play activities for preschool-aged children.

OBJECTIVES

The student will:

- learn about the physical, emotional, social, and mental growth of three- and four-year-olds
- learn and practice the organizational skills needed to set up a playschool for three- and four-year-old children
- plan a set of play activities for three- and four-year-olds based upon their child growth and development knowledge
- practice the principles of good nutrition by planning and serving a nutritious snack during the playschool
- evaluate the playschool experience

TEACHER PREPARATION

1. Make copies of the activity sheets "Playschool," "Characteristics of Three- and Four-Year-Olds," "Am I Three or Am I Four?" "Plan of Action," and "What Did I See?"
2. Identify the three- and four-year-olds who can attend a playschool. Check with members of the class, friends, colleagues, and neighbors.
3. Have textbooks or other references regarding the physical, mental, emotional, and social characteristics of three- and four-year-olds available for use in class.
4. Make a list of toys, art supplies, storybooks, and so on that will be available for students to use in planning the playschool experience.
5. Develop a list of playschool activities from which the students can choose. Have this list duplicated for distribution, place it on an overhead transparency, or prepare a chart to display in the classroom.

6. Divide the class into groups so that you have five or six groups to plan the playschool activities. (See the activity sheet "Plan of Action.")

7. This lesson works best with a double period. If this is not possible, try to make arrangements to have your students excused from their next class for the additional time needed.

ACTIVITIES

Class Period 1

1. Begin this lesson by introducing the idea of a playschool to the students. What is a playschool? What have they learned to date that has prepared them to set up such an experience? What types of things do they need to plan for to set up such an experience? What can they learn from a planned experience with real young children?

   Explain that you will need a group of three- and four-year-olds, usually 10 or 15. Share with the students the reason for selecting this age group. Provide some structure for the later activities by giving students an overview of what they will be doing:
   a. contacting parents and inviting the children
   b. learning more about three- and four-year-olds
   c. deciding the play activities to use with the children during the playschool
   d. completing the organization necessary to hold the playschool
   e. conducting the playschool
   f. completing an evaluation of the playschool experience

2. Distribute the activity sheet "Playschool." Go over this letter of invitation with the students. Identify class members who will be responsible for inviting the participants. Suggest younger brothers or sisters, neighborhood children, children for whom they babysit, children at church, and so on.

   Hold a discussion about what to expect when a group of three- and four-year-olds arrive in a strange classroom. Might some become upset? Why? Might someone not want his or her parent to leave? Why? Will it be helpful if they know one of us? Why? What do we do if a child becomes upset?

3. Verify who will be inviting a child. Review the procedure of delivering the letter and letting the class know who will be coming. Establish a deadline for delivering the invitation.

4. Distribute the activity sheet "Characteristics of Three- and Four-Year-Olds." Point out the whereabouts of the references they are to use in completing the activity sheet. Go over the directions and answer any questions. When the students seem to have finished, conduct a large-group sharing and make a list at the chalkboard or overhead projector. Distribute the activity sheet "Am I Three or Am I Four?" and complete it as a large-group activity.

Class Period 2

1. Begin this class by reviewing what has been completed to date: (a) children to attend have been identified; (b) letters of invitation have been delivered; and (c) we have strengthened our knowledge

of three- and four-year-olds. The next step is to complete the planning and organization necessary for a successful playschool. Assign the students to their planning groups. Provide the class with the list of toys, games, storybooks, art supplies, and so on that will be available for them to use. Explain that there will be a large-group activity that will be decided by the entire class. The other activities will be planned by the small groups.

2. Distribute the activity sheet "Plan of Action." Go over the assignment. The first task is to decide on the centers that will be available during the playschool. Make some suggestions for activities such as a storytelling, cooking, general toy, puzzle, art, music, or snack center. Explain that after each group identifies five possible activities, the actual activities will be decided upon. It may be necessary to compromise because, obviously, only one snack center is needed.

3. When students have completed the above, go over each group's first choice and, through an organized process, decide on what each group will be doing. Ask for ideas for the large-group activity and decide on one. Ask for volunteers to be responsible for the large-group activity.

4. Let the students complete the activity sheet in their small groups. Circulate and help those groups that may have questions or are having difficulty making decisions. All preparations for the playschool should be completed during this class period. Review the activity sheet "What Did I See?" so that students will know what to look for during the playschool.

Class Periods 3 and 4

1. Conduct the playschool according to the prearranged plans. Have students quickly set up their activity centers, greet the children, help them get started, and begin their observations. You may want to greet and talk with the people who brought the children. Take this opportunity to observe your students and evaluate their communication and interaction skills.

2. When the children have gone and the clean-up phase is completed, encourage the students to give a quick reaction to the experience. Have them complete the activity sheet "What Did I See?" in class or as a homework assignment. It is important that they complete this, if at all possible, while the facts are still fresh in their minds.

Class Period 5

1. Discuss the playschool by reviewing the questions on the activity sheet "What Did I See?"

2. Conclude this series of lessons with a discussion of questions such as the following. Why are play activities and toys important to the development of the child? During the playschool, were you able to identify individual differences in children? What were some of them? What type of activities did the class choose for the playschool? Social? Emotional? Mental? Physical? Did any of the playschool activities allow for creativity and imagination? What were they? Was your personal experience with the children an enjoyable one? In what way? Did you gain more self-understanding by studying child growth and development and observing children in action? In what way? Could you see similarities between preschoolers and teenagers in respect to needs and daily problems? Do you feel confident in your knowledge to plan and carry out play activities with young children? How has this helped you understand others?

BACKGROUND INFORMATION

The following is a list of ideas for playschool activities:

a. Buy fruit-flavored cereal, different shapes of macaroni, felt-tip markers, yarn, and transparent tape to make jewelry. Place the tape on the ends of the yarn for easy threading of the "jewels."

b. Make paper bag puppets and tell a story so that the children can use their puppets as characters.

c. Use paper plates to design masks. You need blunt scissors, crayons, markers, and string.

d. Set up a center with cookie cutters, child-sized pots and pans, cutting boards, and play dough.

e. Use old magazines, construction paper, blunt scissors, and glue or paste to create collages.

f. Play dress-up. Have students collect old clothes or costumes for the children to use. Take an instant photo of each dressed-up child so that he or she can take it home.

g. Let children prepare their own snack. Apple faces, instant pudding, small sandwiches, and cheese and crackers are examples of things that work well.

PLAYSCHOOL

Please come!

Our child care class has been studying child development concepts and is going to have a playschool. We are inviting three- and four-year-old children on _____ from _____ to _____. We would very much like your child, _____, to attend.

During the hour your child is with us, there will be organized small-group play and a large-group activity. A nutritious snack or lunch will be provided depending upon the time of the play-school.

Please let us know if your child can attend by completing the form at the bottom of this notice and returning it to us by _____. This activity is being conducted by the Home Economics Department. If you have any questions, please call me at _____. You will be responsible for the child's transportation to and from school.

Thank you very much. We look forward to meeting _____

Sincerely,

_____

Home Economics Teacher

- -

(Cut along dotted line and return this portion to school.)

Child's name _____ Age _____

List any food allergies _____

Home phone number _____

Person to contact in case of emergency _____

Phone number of person to contact in case of emergency _____

_____

Signature of Parent/Guardian

CHARACTERISTICS OF
THREE- AND FOUR-YEAR-OLDS

We have learned that play activities should be suitable to the child's stage of growth and development. Since we are going to invite three- and four-year-old children to a playschool, you need to have information about what they are capable of doing. Read about this age-level child in the references your teacher has provided. Make a list of the physical, emotional, mental, and social characteristics of three- and four-year-old children.

PHYSICAL

_____

_____

_____

_____

EMOTIONAL

_____

_____

_____

_____

MENTAL

_____

_____

_____

_____

SOCIAL

_____

_____

_____

_____

AM I THREE OR AM I FOUR?

Place a 3 or a 4 in front of each statement to identify the age level for that particular characteristic.

_____ 1. Alternates feet going up stairs

_____ 2. Can lace shoes

_____ 3. Cuts on the line with scissors

_____ 4. Rides a tricycle

_____ 5. Can draw a recognizable person or house

_____ 6. Engages in silly play with no carryover from day to day

_____ 7. Can list objects in a picture

_____ 8. Can run and jump, not just jump up and down

_____ 9. Can fashion crude objects from clay

_____ 10. Plays with trucks, trains, and automatic toys

_____ 11. Rides a tricycle for long periods of time

_____ 12. Feeds self with little spilling

_____ 13. Can dress self with easier garments

_____ 14. Likes to play with friends

_____ 15. Can dress and undress

_____ 16. Matches puzzle forms (square, circle, triangle)

_____ 17. Throws overhand with less body participation

_____ 18. Is interested in why things work and relationships

PLAN OF ACTION

List five activities that our class could provide for a group of three- and four-year-old children when they attend our playschool:

1. _____

2 _____

3 _____

4 _____

5. _____

Here is my idea for a large-group activity:

_____

My group has decided to do the following for the playschool:

_____

Materials and equipment needed for the activity:

_____

_____

List of materials to be purchased:

_____

_____

_____

Number of people needed to carry out the

activity: _____
Advance preparations needed:

_____

_____

_____

_____

_____

_____

_____

_____

Name _____   Date _____

WHAT DID I SEE?

Now that the playschool is over, it is important to find out if it was a worthwhile experience for you. One way to do that is to jot down your observations and reactions. Make sure your responses contain enough detail for you to remember exactly what was happening.

1. Describe a child who played well with other children. Why did he or she get along with others?

_____

_____

_____

2. Approximately how many children played alone? _____ What did they do when alone?

_____

_____

_____

_____

3. Under what circumstances did children ask for help?

_____

_____

_____

4. Describe any displays of emotion.

_____

_____

_____

_____

_____

_____

(continued)

WHAT DID I SEE? (continued)

5. Describe ways you saw children display independence.

_____

_____

_____

6. Did you have difficulty understanding the children? _____

7. Describe how teachers got involved when there were cases of poor cooperation.

_____

_____

_____

8. Describe evidences of senses of humor you observed.

_____

_____

_____

9. Was your group well prepared? _____ If not, what would you do differently?

_____

_____

_____

10. On a scale of 1 to 10, with 10 being the most successful, how would you rate the success of the playschool? _____ Why? _____

_____

_____

11. List three things you learned from this experience. Use the back of this sheet if you need more space to write.

_____

_____

_____

_____

_____

_____

_____

MANAGEMENT
AND CONSUMERISM

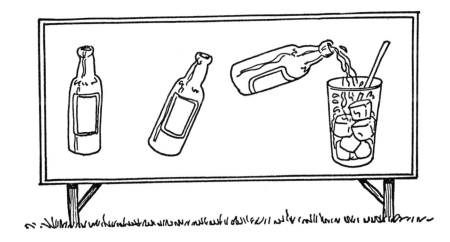

■ DECISION MAKING

CONCEPTS

- Decision makers use a systematic process to arrive at a solution to a problem.
- Decisions are influenced by facts, wants, and needs.
- Decisions concerning similar problems change over time.
- Decisions made by use of a systematic process are usually better decisions.

OBJECTIVES

The student will:

- practice using a decision-making process to select a gift for a friend
- practice using a decision-making process to achieve a personal goal
- learn to distinguish between wants and needs
- identify the factors that influence personal decisions

TEACHER PREPARATION

- Make copies of the activity sheets "The Decision-Making Process," "Making Your Own Decision," and "Making Your Choice."
- Make a list of several examples of decisions teenagers make. Keep them simple, such as a gift for Mother's Day, going for pizza, buying a sweater, going to the movies, staying home to study, and so on.
- Make a transparency of the Decision Wheel.

ACTIVITIES

1. Introduce the decision-making process by describing a decision you recently made. Discuss the factors you considered before arriving at your decision. Did these factors center around certain topics such as time or money? Was your decision satisfactory? Why?
2. Establish the scenario that the students are going to purchase a birthday gift for a friend. Distribute the activity sheet "The Decision-Making Process." Use the transparency of the Decision Wheel

or draw one at the chalkboard to explain the steps in the decision-making process. Have the students make notes on their activity sheet for each step of the process as you explain it. At the conclusion of this exercise, students should notice that people don't always agree on the final decision. Why is that so? Have the students practice making a decision by completing the activity sheet "Making Your Own Decision." When students have finished, let a few describe how they used the decision-making process to come to a decision.

3. Review the directions for completing "Making Your Choice." Clarify any questions students may have about the assignment. Point out that when they get to question seven, they will need to work with a partner.

4. Conclude the lesson by reviewing students' answers to the questions. Spend some time helping students clarify the difference between wants and needs. You can do this by asking someone to look up his or her definition in a dictionary. You can also ask each student to identify each of his or her choices as a want or need and tell why he or she thinks it is so. Are wants and needs the same for all people? Carefully explain why it is important to be able to distinguish a want from a need. Conclude the lesson by restating the basic seven steps of the decision-making process and emphasizing that a systematic decision-making process almost always produces better decisions than the trial-and-error method of problem solving.

THE DECISION-MAKING PROCESS

Every day there are decisions you must make. Many are small, and may involve things like whether you are going to stay in bed an extra minute or eat breakfast. Others are much more important, such as what career you are going to choose.

Fortunately, there are systematic processes we can use to help us make decisions. If we use a systematic process, we can almost always be assured we will make better decisions. One example of such a process is shown below. It is called the Decision Wheel.

Your teacher is going to discuss the Decision Wheel process and apply it to making a selection of a birthday gift for a friend. Follow along, and make notes in each part of the wheel.

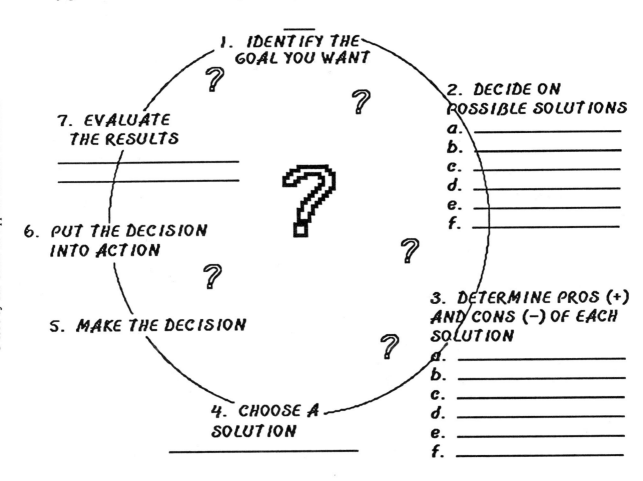

MAKING YOUR OWN DECISION

Your teacher has reviewed the decision-making process called the Decision Wheel. Now it is your turn to try to use the process. Think of a decision you might have to make. Keep it simple. For example, you might want to use as your problem whether or not to go to the movies, or deciding which sweater or jacket to buy, and so on. Complete each section of the wheel.

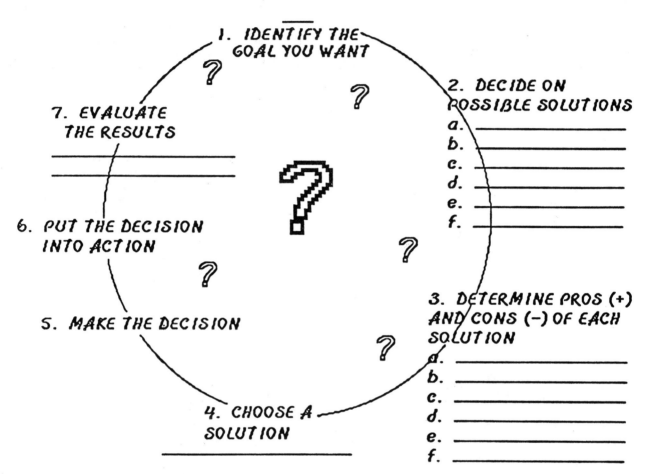

MAKING YOUR CHOICE

Not all of the decisions we have to make are as simple as the one we just practiced. This activity sheet will teach you the steps to use in more complicated decisions. Follow these directions closely.

1. Examine the Calendar of Events shown below. Note that it lists information and events for most days of the month. On the blank calendar, write a plan of action for the entire month by choosing what you are going to do from the Calendar of Events. You may decide to change your mind later. If two options are given, you must make a choice of one of them.

2. List all of your choices that require spending money in the Expenditures column and the actual dollar amount in the $ column in the Balance Sheet section. If you see −$? this means that you must decide on the amount of the expenditure if you choose that activity.

3. Do the same thing for any gains in money you have.

4. Decide if the activity is a ''want'' or a ''need.''

5. Complete the Balance Sheet.

6. Answer the questions about how you made your decision.

(continued)

Sunday	Monday	Tuesday	Wednesday	Thursday	Friday	Saturday
		1 Make own dinner at home (free) OR Eat at Burger Man −$2.50	2 ½ DAY Go to town with friends −$4.00 OR Cut grass +$5.00	3	4 Fun night −$.75	5 Help wash windows +$4.00 OR Go swimming −$2.50
6 BIG SALE! T-shirt −$4.00 Jeans −$14.00 Sandals −$12.00 −$?	7 Favorite Magazine subscription −$6.00	8 Best friend's birthday (gift?) −$?	9 After-school meeting OR Clean basement +$3.50	10 Visit elderly neighbor OR Meet friends for pizza −$2.00	11 Help plant garden +$3.50 OR Go bowling −$2.50	12 Go to track meet to see brother compete −$1.00
13 Go on free trip OR Babysit sister +$4.00	14 Cassette tape sale! $9.50 −$?	15 Parents' anniversary surprise party (gift?) −$?	16 Friend entering "Jump for Heart Health" (sponsor?) −$?	17	18 SCHOOL DANCE admission −$.75 soda −$.50 chips −$.50 −$?	19 Slumber party; bring snack −$2.00 OR Babysit +$8.00
20 Club trip for hiking, picnic, camping −$3.00	21	22 Watch a movie on cable TV at home OR Study	23 Watch favorite TV shows OR Play video games −$?	24 Babysit until 10 P.M. +$5.00 OR Study for test	25 Go to the movies −$3.00 OR Babysit +$6.00	26 Pool party −$4.00 OR Run errands +$3.00
27	28 NO SCHOOL Movie with friends −$3.50 OR Rake garden +$3.00	29 Sister's birthday (gift?) −$?	30 Softball practice OR Babysit +$7.00			

(continued)

130

Name _____   Date _____

MAKING YOUR CHOICE (continued)

Sunday	Monday	Tuesday	Wednesday	Thursday	Friday	Saturday
		1	2	3	4	5
6	7	8	9	10	11	12
13	14	15	16	17	18	19
20	21	22	23	24	25	26
27	28	29	30			

BALANCE SHEET

(−)Expenditures(−)	$	Want	Need	(+)Gains(+)	$	Want	Need
				Allowance	$4.00		

Summary

Total income: _____

Less total expenditures: − _____

FINAL TOTAL: _____

If you decide to put all or part of the money remaining into a savings account, your parents will match that amount with their own money.

Amount to savings: + _____

GRAND TOTAL _____
(Add Final Total and amount to savings)

(continued)

131

MAKING YOUR CHOICE (continued)

1. On which days were the choices hardest? _____

   _____

   Why? _____

   _____

   _____

2. Did you change your choice of activities? _____ What factors caused you to do this? _____

   _____

   _____

3. What problems did you face in coming to a decision? _____

   _____

   _____

   _____

4. Did you have to make comparisons? _____ What were they? _____

   _____

   _____

5 Were you satisfied with your final choice? _____ Why? _____

   _____

   _____

6 Were you budget oriented? Free spending? Flexible? Rigid? Responsible? Irresponsible? Briefly describe

   yourself in terms of these characteristics. _____

   _____

   _____

   _____

   _____

   _____

   _____

   _____

   _____

   _____

© 1990 by The Center for Applied Research in Education

Name _____   Date _____

MAKING YOUR CHOICE (continued)

7. Compare your information with another member of the class. Is your information similar or different? _____ Why? _____

_____

_____

_____

8. What did you learn about yourself and how you make decisions? _____

_____

_____

_____

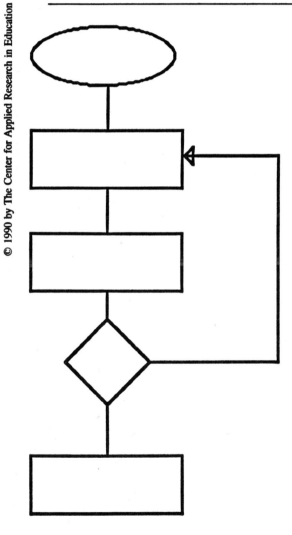

CAN YOU SAY YOU FOLLOW A SYSTEMATIC
PROCESS TO MAKE DECISIONS
OR
DO YOU JUST MAKE A DECISION
AND SEE WHAT HAPPENS?

133

■ ADVERTISING

CONCEPTS

- Consumer decision making is influenced by advertising.
- Advertisers appeal to consumers' emotions.
- Consumers need to identify factual information in advertising.

OBJECTIVES

The student will:

- identify eleven types of advertising appeals and be able to give an example of each
- write a slogan or jingle for an advertisement based upon one of the eleven advertising appeals
- identify the emotional appeal elements in selected advertisements
- identify the factual elements in selected advertisements

TEACHER PREPARATION

- Make copies of the activity sheets "Advertising Appeals," "Finding the 'Hooks,'" and "Write a Jingle" for student use in class.
- Get copies of recent magazines that contain abundant advertising about items with which students are familiar.
- If you plan to use a computer and software to analyze an advertisement, make arrangements to use your school's computer laboratory or have several computers brought to your classroom. You will also need the appropriate software. One example is *Analyzing an Ad* by MCE, Inc., 157 S. Kalamazoo Mall, Kalamazoo, MI 49007.
- Make a decision about whether you want students to work in pairs or individually to write a slogan or jingle. This decision might be dependent upon the students' writing abilities.
- Start a file of advertising appeals. Make sure you include examples of all the types of appeal. The file can be used in the future when students are unable to locate examples for some of the types of appeal.

ACTIVITIES

Option 1

1. Ask students how many advertisements they think they see in one day. What are the advertisements about? What is the purpose of the advertisements? Are advertisements effective? How do we know that? What makes some ads effective and others less so? Can they think of an example of an effective ad? An ineffective one? Do ads contain both straightforward factual information and information that appeals to consumers' emotions? Is it important to know the difference? Why?

   Distribute the activity sheet "Advertising Appeals." Have the students read it. Discuss each appeal, clarify the meaning of each, and seek examples from the students.

2. When you have completed the discussion of the different types of appeal, have the students look through magazines to find four examples from the eleven reviewed. When they have finished completing the activity sheet, discuss the examples students found. Do this in a systematic manner, asking for an example of each type of appeal. Strive to have students be able to distinguish factual information from emotional appeal. Ask students how much consumers are influenced by advertising. How do they know? Are they influenced? By what? Can they give concrete examples of what and why?

   Distribute the activity sheet "Finding the 'Hooks.'" When students have completed identifying the "hooks," ask for student volunteers to share their findings with the class. Ask for examples from each of the eleven categories. Conclude this part of the lesson by pointing out that consumers should be aware of advertising's "pull." If they are not, they may purchase something they do not need. They may end up with a product more expensive or elaborate than they need.

3. Direct the students to the activity sheet "Write a Jingle." Discuss the assignment with them. Clarify any questions. Have students share their examples with the class. Bring the lesson to a close by discussing how advertising can be helpful to consumers. Review how being knowledgeable about advertising helps make consumers immune to its "hooks."

Option 2

This procedure may be substituted for steps 2 and 3 above if your school has microcomputers available. The activity can be completed in your classroom with one or two computers or in your school's computer lab. You will need some software, such as *Analyzing an Ad*. It has two options. In the section "Information About Advertising," a tutorial format is used to present information about broadcast advertising. The "Designing Your Own Ad" section allows the student to select a product, create a slogan, learn about the design of advertisements, and to make a printed copy of the ad he or she designed.

ADVERTISING APPEALS

Advertising is everywhere: television, radio, magazines, newspapers, catalogs, billboards, vehicles, T-shirts, display windows, brochures, and displays set up in stores.

The average person is exposed to more than 75 ads each day. Ads appeal to different emotions. Some of the more popular appeals used in advertising today are described below.

Find examples of at least four of these appeals from the magazines provided. Neatly attach them to a piece of paper. Label each picture as to its appeal. Be prepared to show your ads to the class and discuss their appeals.

INFORMATION   Ads that give simple, direct information are quite often limited to classified ads or general ads for equipment, such as typewriters, lawn mowers, pocket calculators, and so on.

Class example: _____

STATUS   If you use the product, you will be one of those who "made it," one who uses only the best, one who has climbed the ladder of success.

Class example: _____

APPROVAL   If you want more friends who like you better, and you want to have more fun, then use this product.

Class example: _____

GOOD TASTE   By using this product, you show that you're the kind of person who enjoys the finer things of life, that you're really "cool" and relaxed about yourself.

Class example: _____

© 1990 by The Center for Applied Research in Education

ADVERTISING APPEALS (continued)

**HERO
ENDORSEMENT**   These ads are designed to make you feel that if you use the product, you will become more like the well-known person who endorses the product.

Class example: _____

**SEXUAL
ATTRACTION**   If you use the product, members of the opposite sex will fight over your charms. If you don't use it, you will always be a "wallflower."

Class example: _____

JOIN THE GANG   Everybody else is using the product, so why don't you? That's the "pitch" used by this kind of ad.

Class example: _____

ENTERTAINMENT   Some ads, particularly television and radio commercials, are mostly entertainment. But underneath the entertainment, the advertiser wants you to remember the product by association with something you enjoyed.

Class example: _____

INTELLIGENCE   This approach suggests that if you use the product, you are sensible and able to avoid advertising gimmicks. You can make up your own mind about what you want to buy or use.

Class example: _____

INDEPENDENCE   If you use this product, people will know that you think and act for yourself, that you don't care what the rest of the world thinks, that you don't really need popular consumer products, and that you're buying after-shave or suntan lotion because you WANT to.

Class example: _____

**DANGLING
COMPARATIVES**   A much used and possible dangerous device, this appeal uses such statements as "make you 100% healthier" (healthier than WHAT?) or "stop better on wet roads" (better than WHAT?).

Class example: _____

FINDING THE "HOOKS"

You have learned about the emotional appeals found in many advertisements. These appeals are sometimes referred to as "hooks." In your last assignment, you found four advertisements that fit four different advertising appeal categories. Your job now is to identify the "hook" in each advertisement. Complete this chart.

Ad Description	*"Hook"*	*Appeal Classification*

WRITE A JINGLE

Product to be advertised: _____

Jingle: _____

_____

_____

_____

_____

_____

_____

_____

Key words: _____

_____

_____

_____

_____

Which advertising appeal did you use? _____

Why? _____

_____

_____

_____

_____

_____

_____

_____

Is there an emotional "hook" in the jingle? _____ If yes, what is it? _____

_____

_____

_____

_____

■ YOU BE THE JUDGE

CONCEPTS

- Skillful buying lets the consumer's dollar go farther.
- Consumer research/report magazines are useful resources to help make wise purchase decisions.

OBJECTIVES

The student will:

- learn how to use consumer research/report magazines to investigate products
- use consumer research information to rate a selected product
- write a report about the research/rating process

TEACHER PREPARATION

- Make copies of the activity sheets "Time to Research a Product" and "My Report."
- Get copies of *Consumer Reports*, *Consumer's Guide*, *Penny Power*, and *Consumer's Research* magazines for use in class. If your school library does not subscribe to these magazines, your librarian can get them for you via inter-library loan. You will need to allow several weeks for delivery of the magazines.

ACTIVITIES

1. Open the class with a discussion about the influence of advertising on consumer decisions to purchase things. Show students several examples of how advertising provides helpful information. Also, show them how it can be misleading. What can a consumer do to make better decisions about products he or she intends to purchase? If the class does not mention consumer magazines that rate products and do not advertise, distribute sample copies of the magazines mentioned above. If you do not have enough copies to go around, have the class get into small groups. Let the students examine the magazines to see what kind of information they contain. Proceed with an analysis of the contents of the magazines by asking questions about what type of information the magazines contain and why a consumer might be interested in the information. Ask the students how this information would be of value in making a decision.

Distribute the activity sheets "Time to Research a Product" and "My Report." Have the students suggest a product they are interested in knowing about. Review the activity sheet by completing it for the product the students have suggested. Make sure you mention that when students complete their own report, they are only to select a product for which there is a comparison chart in the magazine. Also, review your expectations for the written report they are to complete. Point out that the report is really their conclusion about which product they would buy with the supporting reasons for their decision.

2. When the class has finished the assignment, have the students share their research with the class. You may wish to construct a bulletin board with the students' findings. Conclude the lesson by asking: Are these magazines helpful resources? When would you use them? How would they help you make a decision?

TIME TO RESEARCH A PRODUCT

Now that you know all about consumer research magazines, you are ready to try your skill at researching a product on your own! Part of your research will include writing a brief report. Remember, spelling and rules of grammar always apply!

If you follow the outline below, you will know what to do to get the information you will need to write your report. Keep your notes in the spaces provided. Let's go to work.

Name of product: _____

Brand receiving the highest rating: _____

Price range of products tested: _____

Difference between highest and lowest prices: _____

Advantages of top-rated brand: _____

_____

_____

_____

_____

Disadvantages of top-rated brand: _____

_____

_____

_____

_____

Sources of information: _____

Now go to the activity sheet "My Report" and follow the directions for preparing your summary of findings.

MY REPORT

On the lines below, write a summary paragraph stating the product you would purchase and giving the reasons for your decision.

_____

_____

_____

_____

_____

_____

_____

_____

_____

_____

_____

_____

_____

_____

_____

_____

_____

_____

_____

_____

research notes

NOTES

■ CONSUMER PRODUCT SURVEY

CONCEPTS

- Surveys can be used to collect information about products from consumers.
- Survey information can be used to rank products according to consumer likes and dislikes.
- Teenagers exert an influence on the marketplace because of their buying power.

OBJECTIVES

The student will:

- collect consumer product survey information
- tabulate product survey responses
- rank order of the products surveyed

TEACHER PREPARATION

- Make three copies of the "Consumer Product Survey" for each student.
- Be prepared to discuss the contents of the survey, how the results will be tabulated, and what conclusions will be drawn from the tabulation.
- Determine the beginning and ending times for completing the survey.
- Decide on a system for tabulating and rank ordering the survey results. A process to consider is to have a group of volunteers complete a tally outside of class.

ACTIVITIES

1. Introduce the idea of surveys. What are they? What are they used for? How is the information gathered? Who uses surveys? Who is asked to respond? What are some examples of surveys conducted in your community in the past year?
2. Distribute the activity sheet "Consumer Product Survey." Have students read the survey. Ask them how the results could be used. Explain that they will be collecting information from other students. This information will be used to rank the products in order of preference. They will

also discuss why students chose what they did. How might a store owner use this information? How might a manufacturer use this information?

3. Discuss how the survey will be conducted. Each student will complete a form and then collect the information from two other students. You should mention when they are to begin to collect the data and when it is due. Explain that the second step in the process will be to test the top two brands in each category before a final choice is determined. A report will be prepared and shared with the students who participated in the survey.

   This activity lends itself to total school involvement. Announcements can be made via posters throughout the school, the daily bulletin, daily announcements, and so on.

4. Have students complete their copy of the survey. Clarify any questions they may have.

5. Conclude the session by completing a *class* tally and rank order list. How many selected a particular brand of peanut butter, for example? When the tally is completed, point out that apparently class members have personal likes and dislikes since not everyone chose the same brands. Who would be interested in this information? Is it important for these people to know why people choose what they do? Why?

   You may want to make the transition to the next lesson at this time. Point out to students that consumers should use some form of selection criteria when making purchasing decisions about products and services. Why is this important? How might they go about it? Does anyone know how organizations such as *Consumer Reports* rates products? Explain that in the next class, they will conduct a consumer test of the top two brands selected for each item in the survey. When the tests are completed, the top-rated brand will be identified. Review the process to be used to complete the survey tally and rank order list.

CONSUMER PRODUCT SURVEY

Teenagers are a growing force in the marketplace. What they buy and how they make their decisions is of interest to educators, manufacturers, designers, retailers, and others. Teens spend $46 on the average shopping trip and 22% of those surveyed are shopping every week! (This is according to the "Fourth Annual National Teen Nutrition Research Report," *Forecast for the Home Economist*, March 1988.) Clearly, you and your peers are making consumer decisions that need to be taken seriously.

To assist our class learn more about teenager preferences, we would like you to complete a consumer survey form. You will be asked to choose among several products and state your reasons for your selections.

Our class will tally the results of the surveys. It will then conduct a consumer comparison test of the two brands most frequently selected for each item. After the test is completed, the product rated number one will be identified.

You can receive a report of the results of the survey and consumer comparison test by completing the information at the end of the survey.

Product Survey

Product One
☐ _____
☐ _____
☐ _____

Product Two
☐ _____
☐ _____
☐ _____

Product Three
☐ _____
☐ _____
☐ _____

(continued)

THE CONSUMER PRODUCT SURVEY

Please read each question carefully. Circle the appropriate answer(s). If none of the answers are appropriate for you, please write your own under the category "other."

1. The brand of peanut butter I like best is . . .
   a. Skippy   b. Jif   c. Peter Pan   d. store brand   e. Superman   f. Smuckers

   h. other, please specify _____
   The reason(s) I like this brand is(are) . . .
   a. cost   b. taste   c. texture   d. brand name   e. what has always been purchased

   e. other, please specify _____

2. The brand of potato chips I like best is . . .
   a. Wise   b. Snyder   c. store brand   d. Pringles   e. Gibbles   f. Lays   g. Ruffles

   h. other, please specify _____
   The reasons(s) I like this brand is(are) . . .
   a. cost   b. taste   c. texture   d. brand name   e. what has always been purchased

   f. doesn't break easily   g. other, please specify _____

3. The brand of yogurt I like best, regardless of flavor is . . .
   a. Dannon   b. Breakfast Time   c. store brand   d. Light n' lively   e. Yo Plait   f. Yes

   g. other, please specify _____

   The reason(s) I like this brand is(are) . . .
   a. flavor   b. texture   c. cost   d. variety of flavors   e. size of fruit   f. brand name

   g. what has always been purchased   h. other, please specify _____

4. The brand of orange juice I like best is . . .
   a. Minute Maid   b. Five Alive   c. Donald Duck   d. Tang   e. store brand   f. Awake

   g. Citrus Hill   h. other, please specify _____
   The reason(s) I like this brand is(are) . . .
   a. flavor   b. texture   c. cost   d. color   e. brand name   f. what has always been purchased   g. other, please specify _____

5. The brand of canned peaches I like best is . . .
   a. Del Monte   b. Cohort   c. store brand   d. other, please specify _____
   The reason(s) I like this brand is(are) . . .
   a. cost   b. color   c. flavor   d. texture   e. amount of syrup   f. brand name   g. what
   has always been purchased   g. other, please specify _____

6. The brand of tissues I like best is . . .
   a. Kleenex   b. Scott   c. Puffs   d. store brand   e. Softie   f. other, please
   specify _____

THE CONSUMER PRODUCT SURVEY (continued)

The reason(s) I like this brand is(are) . . .
a. softness   b. strength   c. colors   d. cost   e. number per box   f. brand name

g. what has always been purchased   h. other, please specify _____

7. The brand of paper towels I like best is . . .
a. Bounty   b. Viva   c. Rally   d. store brand   e. other, please specify _____
The reason(s) I like this brand is(are) . . .
a. absorbency   b. strength   c. cost   d. quantity per roll   e. brand name   f. what has

always been purchased   g. other, please specify _____

8. The brand of hand lotion I like best is . . .
a. Jergens   b. Vaseline Intensive Care   c. store brand   d. Avon   e. other, please specify

_____

The reason(s) I like this brand is(are) . . .
a. greaseless   b. absorbed quickly   c. makes hands feel soft   d. brand name   e. smell

f cost   g. what has always been purchased   g. other, please specify _____

THANK YOU FOR COMPLETING THIS SURVEY. Please add your name and homeroom number
if you would like to receive a copy of the results of the survey.

_____ NAME

_____ HOMEROOM

■ PRODUCT COMPARISONS

CONCEPTS

- Product comparisons can lead to making wiser purchases.

OBJECTIVES

The student will:

- compare products using a set of descriptors
- choose from a selection of products and state the reason(s) for the choice

TEACHER PREPARATION

- Collect and review the survey tally and rank order list.
- Purchase the two brands of each item most frequently selected on the "Consumer Product Survey." Be sure to keep a record of the unit cost of each item. You will also need paper plates, cups, plastic forks and spoons, and napkins.
- Organize the eight testing centers. The center should include the products to be compared. To disguise the brand name and price of the products, place chips, peaches, and yogurt in appropriate-size bowls. Squeeze hand lotion into small dishes, too. Tissues can be taken out of the boxes and placed in separate piles. Wrap the peanut butter jars in construction paper. Just removing the wrappers from paper towels will do the job. The orange juice should be made up in a pitcher. You will need to label each product as Brand A and Brand B. Place enough plates, cups, plastic utensils, and napkins in each center for each student to perform necessary taste tests.
- Prepare a master sheet that lists the name for each Brand A and Brand B along with its price.
- Make copies of the activity sheet "Product Comparisons."
- Make an overhead transparency of "Product Comparisons."

ACTIVITIES

1. Distribute the activity sheet "Product Comparisons" and review the task outlined. Explain that students are going to compare the two most frequently selected brands of each of the eight products.

Point out this comparison test is not scientific, but it is an example of how people can use information to make wiser selections.

2. Have the students complete their comparisons.

3. When everyone has finished the comparisons, point out that they made their choices not knowing the cost of the products. Would they normally do that? Is cost a factor? Should it be a factor? What is the best way to compare cost? (unit cost) Divulge the unit cost of each product and have the students write it in the appropriate space. Also have them compute the difference and note it in the space provided. Have the students check their notes about each product as you ask the question, "Would the difference in the cost have altered your decision? Why or why not?"

4. Complete a tally of the brand name chosen for each product. You can add some interest to this activity by having the students guess the brand names for each product before you divulge it. Discuss the reasons why students chose each product. Was the set of descriptors useful in accurately making a decision about which was the best product? Why or why not? How could they use this process to make better selections of products?

5. To bring this lesson to a close, ask the class if they agreed with the survey respondents as to which brands are best. Could our survey/comparison information be useful to a manufacturer? How? Could it be useful to local stores? How? Did you remain loyal to "your" brand? Why? Were you influenced by other people during the product-testing process? Does peer pressure affect the acceptance of various products? How? Would you enjoy being a product tester? In order to compare products, what does the tester need to know? Can this process be used in other consumer decisions? What consumer decisions? Students should be left with the knowledge that smart consumers take the time to examine products with some set of criteria. They get more for their money, a better product, and, generally, fall for fewer compulsive shopper traps.

PRODUCT COMPARISONS

Many people select the products they purchase after making comparisons of the products available. We have completed a survey to determine which of several products students in our school prefer. We are now going to submit the two most preferred products in each category to a comparison test.

Examine the charts below. You will see that the desirable qualities for each product are given in a list of descriptors at the top of the chart. Your task is to examine each product—look at it, smell it, taste it, touch it—whatever you need to do to evaluate the categories listed for each. Make notes of your opinions in the spaces provided. Before you leave the testing center, indicate your choice of brand and state the reason(s) for your decision.

PEANUT BUTTER

Top-quality peanut butter should look smooth in texture and have a light brown color with only a trace of oil. It should taste and smell like roasted peanuts. It can taste and smell sweet, but should not be too sweet. There should only be a hint of saltiness. There should be no stale or rancid taste.

Brand A	Brand B
Appearance:	Appearance:
Aroma:	Aroma:
Flavor:	Flavor:
Texture:	Texture:

(continued)

PRODUCT COMPARISONS (continued)

My choice is Brand _____. I chose it because _____

_____

The cost of Brand A is _____. The cost of Brand B is _____. The cost difference is

_____.

POTATO CHIPS

Top-quality potato chips should be crisp with a hint of salt. They should not leave an excessive greasy coating or taste of salt in your mouth. The color should be light yellow with no green edges. They should not smell or taste stale or rancid.

Brand A	*Brand B*
Appearance:	Appearance:
Aroma:	Aroma:
Flavor:	Flavor:
Texture:	Texture:

My choice is Brand _____. I chose it because _____

_____

The cost of Brand A is _____. The cost of Brand B is _____. The cost difference is

_____.

(continued)

PRODUCT COMPARISONS (continued)

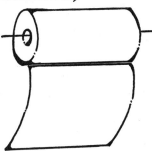

PAPER TOWELS

Towels should be strong, absorbent, and leave no streaks when used to clean glass.

Brand A	*Brand B*
Texture:	Texture:
Absorbency:	Absorbency:
Strength:	Strength:

My choice is Brand _____. I chose it because _____

_____

The cost of Brand A is _____, The cost of Brand B is _____. The cost difference is

_____.

TISSUES

A quality tissue should be soft to the touch, resistant to moisture, and survive a sneeze. The scent should be mild and pleasant.

Brand A	*Brand B*
Softness:	Softness:

PRODUCT COMPARISONS (continued)

Wet strength:	Wet strength:
Scent:	Scent:

My choice is Brand _____. I chose it because _____

_____

The cost of Brand A is _____. The cost of Brand B is _____. The cost difference is

_____.

HAND LOTION

Top-quality hand lotion should be smooth, absorbed into the skin quickly, and leave no greasy coating on the skin. The scent should be light.

Brand A	*Brand B*
Absorbency:	Absorbency:
Texture:	Texture:
Scent:	Scent:

PRODUCT COMPARISONS (continued)

My choice is Brand _____. I chose it because _____

_____

The cost of Brand A is _____. The cost of Brand B is _____. The cost difference is

_____.

YOGURT

Yogurt should have some astringency as well as a sweet-sour character. It should have a clean, pleasant aftertaste and slightly coat the mouth. It should have a creamy consistency with visible bits of fruit (if fruit-flavored).

Brand A	Brand B
Appearance:	Appearance:
Aroma:	Aroma:
Flavor:	Flavor:
Texture:	Texture:

My choice is Brand _____. I chose it because _____

_____

The cost of Brand A is _____. The cost of Brand B is _____. The cost difference is

_____.

(continued)

PRODUCT COMPARISONS (continued)

ORANGE JUICE

Top-quality orange juice should smell and taste like fresh oranges. It should have a zesty flavor that comes from the peel. No off flavor or bitterness should be present. There should be evidence of fruit pulp. The color should be a uniform light orange.

Brand A	Brand B
Appearance:	Appearance:
Aroma:	Aroma:
Flavor:	Flavor:
Texture:	Texture:

My choice is Brand _____. I chose it because _____

The cost of Brand A is _____. The cost of Brand B is _____. The cost difference is

_____.

PEACHES

Sliced peaches should have a slightly firm texture with a yellow to orange color. They should have a sweet taste, but not be overpowered by the syrup. There should be no off flavor or bitter taste.

(continued)

PRODUCT COMPARISONS (continued)

Brand A	*Brand B*
Appearance:	Appearance:
Aroma:	Aroma:
Flavor:	Flavor:
Texture:	Texture:

My choice is Brand _____. I chose it because _____

_____

The cost of Brand A is _____. The cost of Brand B is _____. The cost difference is

_____.

■ FOOD PROCESSING AND PACKAGING COSTS

CONCEPTS

- Consumers should be concerned about the cost of packaging and processing food products.
- Processing and packaging food products affect their cost to the consumer.
- Processing and packaging food products consume energy in several different forms.
- Food packaging materials can have a negative impact upon the environment and should be considered as a cost.

OBJECTIVES

The student will:

- learn that the dollar cost of food products is significantly affected by packaging and processing
- compare the costs of processed food products with products made from scratch
- become aware of the negative environmental impact of certain packaging materials
- analyze the energy and environmental costs of fast food products

TEACHER PREPARATION

- Make copies of "Energy Costs," "Environmental Impact," "Costs Compared," and "Personal Costs."
- Have calorie and nutrient analysis charts from one of your textbooks or reference books ready for student use.
- Obtain a box from a TV dinner that includes meat, potatoes, and peas; the wrapper from ready-to-eat rolls; and the package from a frozen fruit pie.
- Determine the prices for Meals A and B described in the activity sheet "Costs Compared." Write these on the chalkboard, on a chart, or on an overhead transparency.

ACTIVITIES

1. Begin this lesson with a discussion of the segments that constitute the total cost of the food products we purchase. Is it the food itself? Who pays for the packaging? Processing? Preparation?

What types of packaging are available? Have you ever purchased anything that was packaged in more than one container? Is there fancy packaging? Plain packaging? Does the difference affect the quality of the product? How? How does this affect the cost to the consumer? What energy costs are involved in bringing frozen foods to market? What happens to the nutrient value of food products each time they are processed? Is this a cost? Has the fast food industry increased our problem with waste management? How? The intent of this discussion is to get students to think about all of the different sources of cost in food products. Conveniences come at a cost. Are there occasions when it is worth the cost? Not worth the cost?

2. Distribute the activity sheet "Energy Cost." You may want to have students complete this task independently, in small groups, or as a large group discussion. The task is to jot down every activity that requires energy consumption in processing a package of frozen french fries from field to home. The conclusion is, of course, that the cost of food products is significantly affected by the cost of the energy involved in processing, packaging, transportation, and storage.

   Point out that these costs are the obvious ones. There are other costs that are not so apparent. We sometimes call these "social costs."

3. Distribute the activity sheet "Environmental Costs." Discuss the National Park Service information. Ask students what significance this has for their environment. Use an overhead projector transparency or chalkboard to record students' analysis of the environmental impact of the packaging involved in a trip to a local fast food restaurant. Multiply this by the millions—what impact are we making on our environment locally, nationally, worldwide? Is there a cost involved? What is it?

4. Distribute the activity sheet "Costs Compared." Review the prices for Meals A and B you have calculated. Briefly go over the assignment and have students complete it. When they have finished, go over their answers. Conclude this section of the lesson by pointing out that consumers have a lot to consider in making food purchases. What is the original cost? Am I getting the most nutrition for my money? Am I harming the environment?

   The final section of this lesson is an analysis of the personal costs involved in making food product purchase decisions.

5. Distribute "Personal Costs," briefly review the task, and have students complete the activity sheet. When they are finished, go over their responses. Point out that there are personal reasons involved in purchasing prepackaged, processed food products. Making food from scratch is not always the best alternative. The key to smart consumer decisions is to think through all of the costs being paid and choosing the least expensive product to do what we want, when, and how we want it.

6. Conclude this lesson by letting students complete the activity sheet "Summarizing." If your class has difficulty with their writing skills, you can assign students to teams, or conduct a large group discussion using an overhead projector and transparency to record class comments. Otherwise, let students complete the activity sheet on their own. When students are finished, have them share their conclusions with the class. Use this opportunity to reinforce the concepts taught in this lesson.

ENERGY COSTS

When we fill our shopping cart at the supermarket, we are not only paying for food products, but we are also paying for the cost of their packaging and processing. The same is true for foods purchased at a fast food restaurant or a take-out establishment. The costs can be measured in dollars, energy consumption, and impact upon the environment.

It is possible to pay as much for a single quarter-pound hamburger as a pound of ground beef. The difference in cost is not in the ground beef, but in the form it has taken due to processing and packaging. Wise consumers ask, "Exactly what is the difference? Is it worth the extra cost?"

A major component of the cost of food products we purchase today is the consumption of energy. Energy costs are involved in production, transportation to market, processing, packaging, and storing. In this lesson, we are only concerned about costs related to processing and packaging.

Part I:

Consider a simple processed food—frozen french fries. List below those steps in the process of getting a package of frozen french fries from the field to the home where energy consumption is involved. Mark those that are processing or packaging with an asterisk (*). If you need more space to write, use the back of this sheet.

_____

_____

_____

_____

_____

_____

Part II:

Does the processing and packaging of frozen french fries affect their price? _____ How? _____

_____

_____

_____

_____

Name _____   Date _____

ENVIRONMENTAL IMPACT

A cost often overlooked is the cost of disposing of the packaging materials. Some of these costs cannot be measured directly in terms of dollars. According to the National Park Service, it requires different amounts of time for different types of litter to decompose. For example:

Paper	2.5 months
Orange peels	6 months
Milk cartons	5 years
Filter-tip cigarette butts	10 to 12 years
Plastic bags	10 to 20 years
Leather shoes	25 to 40 years
Nylon cloth	30 to 40 years
Plastic containers	50 to 80 years
Aluminum	80 to 100 years
Plastic foam	Never

Part I:

Imagine you have taken a trip to your neighborhood fast food restaurant. You have ordered a burger with fries, a large soft drink, and a hot fudge sundae. In terms of time to dispose of the waste, what is the cost of the packaging?

_____

_____

_____

_____

_____

_____

Part II:

Is this high-cost packaging? _____ Why? _____

_____

Part III:

Would you support a ban on nonbiodegradable packaging? _____ Why? _____

_____

_____

_____

COSTS COMPARED

It is important for consumers to compare the cost of food products in different forms. Smart consumers compare both dollar costs and nutritional costs. They consider such questions as the following: Did the act of processing the food alter its nutritional value? Is the convenience worth the extra dollar cost? Is the convenience worth the loss of nutritional value? Is the added nutritional value worth the extra cost?

Look at the two menus below. Compare them.

Meal A	*Meal B*
TV dinner (meat, potatoes, peas)	bean soup (homemade from dried
ready-to-eat rolls	beans)
frozen fruit pie	ham sandwich
milk	tossed salad
	fresh fruit with cheese
	water

1. I think Meal _____ is more energy costly because _____

_____

2. I think Meal _____ costs more because _____

3. I think Meal _____ would take more time to prepare. It is a price I would be willing to pay if _____

_____

4. I think Meal _____ has more nutrients because _____

_____

5. I think Meal _____ has more calories.

6. I think Meal _____ has more environmental impact because _____

_____

Foods contain "leader" nutrients and calories. Leader nutrients are those that occur in the largest amount. For example, vitamins A and C are leader nutrients in orange juice. Use a nutrient analysis and calorie chart to determine the leader nutrients and number of calories in each meal.

7. Meal A has _____ calories and _____

_____ nutrients.

8. Meal B has _____ calories and _____

_____ nutrients.

9. Which meal is the better dollar value? _____ Why? _____

_____

Name _____ Date _____

PERSONAL COSTS

Not all costs related to food products can be measured in terms of dollars for packaging and processing or impact on the environment. There are personal costs involved that a consumer should take into consideration. For example, how much time does he or she have available for food preparation? How does the consumer like to spend his or her free time?

Consider Consumer A and Consumer B. Their meals were described on the activity sheet "Costs Compared."

Consumer A speaks: "I chose my meal because I'm busy and I don't like to cook. I know it costs more, but I think I can afford and justify the extra cost. My preference is to put something in the oven and relax while it cooks. I use my microwave a lot because it saves me a lot of time. I'm aware that some vitamins are lost in cooking because the TV dinners are cooked twice. I'll make up for that by taking a vitamin supplement each day."

Consumer B speaks: "I'm worried about ecology in our country. I think I can help by not buying food products packaged in containers that have a negative impact on the environment. I know it takes a lot of energy to produce throw-away TV dinner and other processed food containers. I'm aware of the energy costs of both processing and storing many convenience foods. As one person, I can't do a great deal, but I want to do my part. I enjoy growing some of my own vegetables and fruits. I am careful to select energy efficient food products when I go to the store. I enjoy cooking and use those techniques that preserve the nutrient value of the food. I combine many of my cooking tasks so that I use time efficiently. For example, I washed and sorted the beans while preparing breakfast and left them to soak and then cooked them at lunchtime. All I had to do for dinner was add spices and seasonings, put them through the blender, and reheat. My meal was low calorie, just the way I like it! If I wanted TV-type dinners, I would cook a little extra at some meals, and make them up into dinners. The trays could be saved and used again. They would be prepared to my sanitary standards. My storage costs would be low because I would plan to use them in the immediate future. My energy costs would be low."

1. What energy services did Consumer A purchase? _____

_____

_____

2. What energy services did Consumer B purchase? _____

_____

_____

3. Which consumer made the "right" decision? Why did you answer this way? _____

_____

_____

_____

_____

(continued)

PERSONAL COSTS (continued)

Values enter into our decisions about which food products we purchase. This can be illustrated by considering two additional costs: the cost of serving and the cost of cleaning up. Read what Consumer A and Consumer B have to say about these matters.

Consumer A speaks: "I don't like to make a big fuss about meals, so I just put the TV trays on the table along with a paper napkin. I very often use plastic throw-away eating utensils. When I'm finished—voila!—into the garbage. No dishwashing! No hot water, no detergent, and hardly any of my precious time. Just the way I like it. I'm doing my part for energy conservation—saved all these things, plus I didn't have to wash and iron a tablecloth and napkins, and didn't use any water in the process. I read that hot water takes fifteen percent of all the energy used in the home. I'd say I did a good job."

Consumer B speaks: "I like to serve meals with elegance. Give me the nice tablecloth with matching napkins and set the table with soup bowls, salad plates, dessert dishes, and water goblets. Now, that's living! After dinner, I put the linens in the laundry, rinse the dishes in hot running water, and put them in the dishwasher. I couldn't stand to throw away valuable resources like disposable dishes, paper napkins, plastic eating utensils, and so on. Such a waste!"

4. In regard to serving and cleaning up, I think Consumer _____ used more energy because _____

_____

_____

5. How did values influence these consumers' decisions? _____

_____

_____

_____

_____

6. Which consumer made the better energy decision regarding the serving and cleaning up costs?

_____ Why? _____

_____

_____

_____

_____

SUMMARIZING

You can see from our discussion that there are many costs involved in providing food products to the consumer. The consumer should be aware of which of these are unavoidable and which are related to convenience. The consumer needs to be aware that convenience comes at a cost. The consumer needs to weigh all of the costs in making a decision about what is best for him or her. The consumer needs to know that there are some hidden costs that impact upon the environment and that should be considered.

Think back over this lesson. Select one or two processing and packaging energy costs that you think are important. Write a brief paragraph explaining why you think they are important and how you, as a consumer, plan to take these costs into consideration in making food product purchases.

_____

_____

_____

_____

_____

_____

_____

_____

_____

_____

_____

_____

_____

_____

_____

_____

_____

_____

_____

_____

_____

■ HOW TO GET ACTION

CONCEPTS

- There is an accepted procedure for consumers to follow to seek redress for faulty goods or services.
- The complaint process starts with a business letter seeking redress.
- A letter of complaint should state all of the facts and specifically state the redress sought.
- There are organizations available to the consumer for help in settling complaints about faulty goods or services.

OBJECTIVES

The student will:

- learn the content to include in a letter of complaint
- review the correct form of a business letter
- write an appropriate letter seeking redress for a faulty product or service
- outline a course of action for the consumer when the manufacturer or business providing a service does not make good on faulty goods or services

TEACHER PREPARATION

- Make copies of "How to Get Action," "Practice Makes it Effective," "One More Time," and "It's Not Over 'Til It's Over."
- Identify consumer action lines or bureaus for your community. Obtain copies of their publications.

ACTIVITIES

1. Briefly discuss the purpose of this lesson. What can a consumer do if a product or service turns out to be faulty or unsatisfactory? Is there a "right" way to go about seeking redress? Distribute the activity sheet "How to Get Action" and have the students read John F. Kennedy's letter to his father. Ask the students if they would have increased his allowance. Why or why not? What made the letter effective or ineffective? Review what should be included in a letter seeking redress and have the students fill in the blanks on the activity sheet.

2. Distribute the activity sheet "Practice Makes It Effective." Have the students read the directions. Clarify any questions. Have the students complete the task. When the students have completed their rewrite, conduct a brief discussion of the corrections that they made. It is important you stress the "why" about what is included in the letter. Students need to see that the consumer has a responsibility to clearly state all of the facts about the problem if he or she is to have it resolved satisfactorily.

3. The next activity, "One More Time," can be used for additional practice in class, as a homework assignment, or as a quiz. When the students have completed the task, collect their papers and correct them. Follow your normal procedure of reviewing students' written assignments.

4. Lead the class in a discussion of what to do if a consumer does not get satisfaction when seeking redress for a faulty product or unsatisfactory service. Distribute the activity sheet "It's Not Over 'Til It's Over" and have the students complete the assignment. When they have finished, have several volunteers share their plan with the class. Point out that consumers should use the same care in approaching another agency as they did with the manufacturer of the product or provider of the service.

5. Conclude the lesson by briefly reviewing the steps responsible consumers take in seeking redress for faulty products and services.

EXTENSION ACTIVITIES

This lesson lends itself to several appropriate extension activities. Some examples are the following:

1. Invite representatives from local consumer advocate groups to share with the class what consumers can do to seek redress for faulty products and services.

2. Set up a panel discussion with representatives of local businesses, industries, and consumer groups to discuss consumer rights and responsibilities in matters of alleged faulty products and services.

3. Schedule your school's computer laboratory to let students practice word processing to complete the assignments for this lesson.

Name _____ Date _____

HOW TO GET ACTION

Read the following letter:

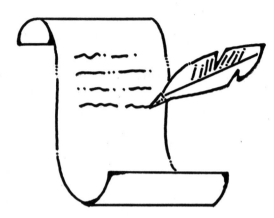

"My recent allowance is 40¢. This I used for aeroplanes and other playthings of childhood but now I am a scout and I put away my childish things. Before I would spend 20¢ of my 40¢ allowance and in five minutes I would have empty pockets and nothing to gain and 20¢ to lose. When, I a scout, I have to buy canteens, haversacks, blankets, searchlights, poncho things that will last for years and I can always use it while I can't use a cholcolate marshmellow sunday with vanilla ice cream and so I put in my plea for a raise of 30¢ for me to buy scout things and pay my own way more around. Finis."

In 1929, after this plea was written by 12-year-old John F. Kennedy, his father, Joseph P. Kennedy, did raise his son's allowance to 70¢. The author of this letter was successful in achieving his goal.

Consumers buy goods and services that turn out to be defective or unsatisfactory. How can they get action? What is the best way to register a complaint? One tested way is to write a letter clearly stating your complaint and the satisfaction you desire.

The following information should be included in a letter to seek redress for a faulty product or unsatisfactory service:

1. Explain the problem _____ and _____.

2. State _____ and _____ you bought the _____ or arranged for the _____.

3. Explain exactly how the product is _____.

4. Give as much specific information as possible, including _____ _____, _____ _____, _____ _____, _____, and _____.

5. List the _____ you have already taken in an attempt to _____ _____ _____.

6. State what you believe should be done about your _____.

7. Include _____, not originals, of supporting papers such as _____, bills, and so on.

8. Keep a _____ of your letter of complaint.

9. If you write a _____ letter, enclose a _____ of the _____ letter.

10. Include the _____ date you will wait for a response before taking _____ step to seek redress.

11. State what your _____ step will be; what you will do; _____ you will contact.

12. Last, but far from least, use the correct form of a business letter. The letter should include: the _____ address, the _____ address, a _____, the _____ of the letter, the _____ close, and your _____.

PRACTICE MAKES IT EFFECTIVE

There is an old saying, "Practice makes perfect." This is certainly true when it comes to writing letters seeking redress for faulty products or services you have purchased. Experience has shown that consumers are more likely to get satisfaction if they include certain specific information. You have just discussed what to include.

Study the letter below. Did the individual follow the guidelines for complaining effectively? Can you improve the letter?

Rewrite the letter so that all of the important information needed by the manufacturer is included. Use the space provided on "The Rewrite."

26 Valleyview Hill
Grafton, NH 12345
January 10, 1991

Temple's Department Store
206 East 3rd Avenue
Mantua, NH 19876

Dear Sir or Madam:

In December, I bought your can opener at Temple's Department Store. It doesn't work well at all

I took it back to the store but they wouldn't give me any satisfaction.

I hope you can do something about it.

Sincerely,

Paul Black

You may want to do some editing by making changes on the actual letter before completing the rewrite on the "The Rewrite" page.

Return Address

space

Address

Salutation

Body

Closing

Name

THE REWRITE

_____

_____

_____

_____

_____

_____

_____

_____

_____

_____

_____

_____

_____

_____

_____

_____

_____

_____

_____

_____

_____

_____

_____

_____

_____

_____

_____

_____

_____

_____

ONE MORE TIME

Six weeks ago, you saw a television advertisement for an ''Easy Does It'' exercise machine. The machine was sold with a money-back guarantee. It cost $49.95 plus $8.00 shipping. You ordered one from the Lazy Day Exercycle Company, 2600 Gotcha Lane, Buyerbeware, OK 98765. When it arrived today, you found several bolts were missing. You could not assemble it. You also found a hairline crack in one of the handlebars.

Decide on what redress you want and write an appropriate letter. Use the back of this sheet if you need more space for your letter.

_____

_____

_____

_____

_____

_____

_____

_____

_____

_____

_____

_____

_____

_____

_____

_____

_____

_____

_____

_____

_____

_____

_____

_____

IT'S NOT OVER 'TIL IT'S OVER

You wrote your letter to Temple Department Store seeking redress and—NOTHING HAS HAPPENED! No redress, no satisfaction. You are right where you started, stuck with an unsatisfactory can opener. Is there anything else you can do? Is there something like a "Last Court of Appeal"? The answer is YES.

If all else fails, there is another step you can take. You can write or call your local Better Business Bureau; the "Action Line" of your local newspaper, radio station, or television station; the Department of Consumer Affairs for your town or state; or the President of the company that sold or manufactured the product. Unsafe products can be reported to the Consumer Product Safety Commission at 1–800–648–8326.

Describe in the space below what you plan to do about the faulty can opener. Use the back of this sheet if you need more space to write.

_____

_____

_____

_____

_____

_____

_____

_____

_____

_____

_____

_____

_____

_____

_____

_____

_____

_____

_____

_____

_____

TEXTILES AND CLOTHING

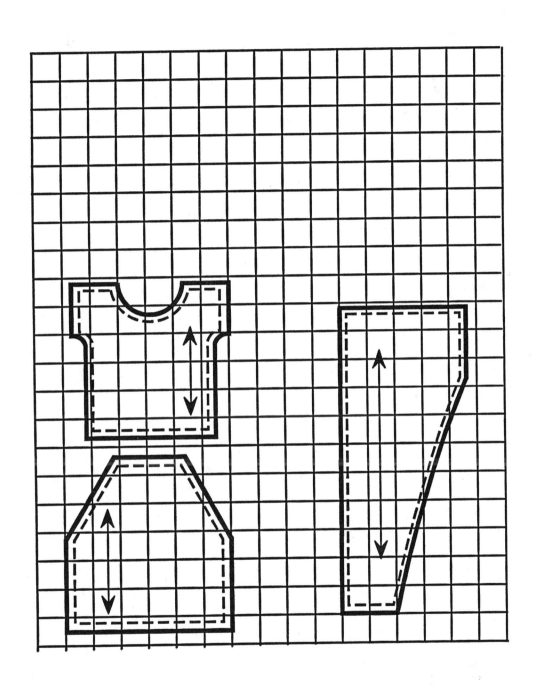

■ THE HISTORY OF TEXTILES

CONCEPTS

- Societal needs influenced the development of textiles.

OBJECTIVES

The student will:

- learn about the major events in the history of textiles
- identify ten major events in the history of textiles and hypothesize as to the need that led to the event

TEACHER PREPARATION

- Make copies of the activity sheets "Events in Textile History" and "The Top Ten Events."
- Collect swatches of cotton, linen, silk, wool, rayon, nylon, orlon, fiberglass, and other synthetic fabrics along with pictures of weaving looms, spinning wheels, the cotton gin, the "flying" shuttle, and modern-day looms and an example of a microchip.
- Prepare a transparency of the "Events in Textile History" list. (See Appendix B for a blackline master.)

ACTIVITIES

1. Begin this lesson with a free-ranging discussion of textiles, the process of making fabric from fiber, and the technological inventions that were developed through the ages. Questions similar to these will open the discussion: What are textiles? What are textiles made from? What are they used for? How did early people make fabric? How is it made today? Can anyone think of any inventions that improved the production of fabrics? What were they? Are all fabrics made from natural fibers? If not, what are they made from? What are examples of natural fabrics? Synthetics? Has the advent of computer technology impacted on the textile industry? How? Illustrate your discussion with samples of fabric and pictures.
2. Distribute the activity sheet "Events in Textile History." Use the "Events in Textile History" transparency to focus students' attention during your discussion. Spend some time reviewing this chart in chronological order.

3. Continue the lesson by having the students complete the activity sheet "Top Ten Events in the History of Textiles."

4. When the students have finished the task above, have them share their selections. At the overhead projector or the chalkboard, compile a class list of the top events. When this is completed, discuss the changes or needs that may have caused these events to occur. It is important for students to understand that most technological developments do not just happen accidentally. They occur because of an unmet need or because of some change in society. A list of the societal changes that influenced the history of textiles would include the following: the increase in the world's population, the rise of cities, the increase in world trade, discoveries in other fields such as chemistry, the spread of wealth to more people, and so on. Have students note the reasons behind the major events in the space provided.

5. Tell students that the next topic they will discuss is the clothing industry. What changes have taken place in the way clothing is manufactured? How are clothes produced today?

EVENTS IN TEXTILE HISTORY

The history of textiles is ancient. No one knows for sure when the first cloth or fabric was discovered by man. Can you think of a need early people had that could have led to the invention of cloth? Certainly protection from the elements had to be one of their earliest needs. They needed fabric from which to make articles of clothing to protect their bodies from the extremes of temperature and various forms of precipitation. As you review this list, try to think of reasons why certain events in the development of textiles might have taken place. Is history an accident? That is the question!

PREHISTORIC AND ANCIENT TIMES

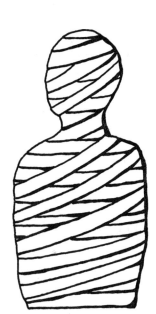

6300 B.C. . . . . Archaeological discovery of fine woven cloth fragments in Turkey (30 to 38 threads per inch).

3000 B.C. . . . . Cotton was being grown in Pakistan, western India, and perhaps the Americas.

2700 B.C. . . . . Chinese cultivated silkworms and developed special looms to weave silk cloth.

2500 B.C. . . . . Linen found on Egyptian mummy woven at 540 ends per inch, as well made as that of today. Goddess Isis shown in a pictograph holding a shuttle.

327 B.C. . . . . Alexander the Great amazed at the beautiful printed cotton being produced in India.

300 B.C. . . . . Ancient Greeks and Romans developed an enormous trade in textiles.

75 B.C. . . . . Silk became the luxury cloth in Rome.

63 B.C. . . . . Cotton awnings were used in Rome.

THE MIDDLE AGES

400–1500 A.D. . . . . . Textile industry gradually developed in Europe.

768 A.D. . . . . Charlemagne established silk weaving industry at Lyons and imported wool from England.

900 . . . . Alfred the Great encouraged expansion of the wool industry in England.

1120 . . . . Henry I sponsored the first woolen cloth guild. He relocated skilled Flemish weavers to English villages to increase production.

(continued)

EVENTS IN TEXTILE HISTORY (continued)

1153 . . . . First annual cloth fair held in England.

1200 . . . . Spinning wheel was in common use.

1305 . . . . Venice had 17,000 people engaged in weaving wool.

1533 . . . . Pizarro reported that Peruvian spinning and weaving was superior to European.

1589 . . . . William Lee invented machine to knit hosiery.

1631 . . . . Dutch East India Company imported fine calico from India.

Early 1600s . . . . . . Textile workers in the Netherlands improved methods of dyeing and finishing cloth.

1654 . . . . English textile craftsmen were forbidden to emigrate to America.

1661 . . . . A resident of Danzig, Poland, built a power loom. (See the illustration.) The government had him drowned and destroyed the loom.

1667 . . . . English law required all persons to be buried in woolen cloth. More cloth was being produced than could be sold.

1669 . . . . The English colonies in America were forbidden from trading wool materials.

1696 . . . . Irish weavers produced cloth less expensively than the English. Attempts were made to suppress the weavers. Irish linen was superior to all others.

1733 . . . . John Kay, an Englishman, invented the flying shuttle loom. (See the illustration.)

1764 . . . . James Hargreaves invented the spinning jenny, the first machine to spin more than one piece of yarn at a time.

1768 . . . . Spinning and weaving contests held in America to oppose the Stamp Act.

1769 . . . . Richard Arkwright patented the water frame, a spinning machine that ran on water power.

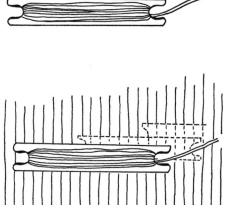

© 1990 by The Center for Applied Research in Education

(continued)

EVENTS IN TEXTILE HISTORY (continued)

1779 . . . .   Samuel Crompton invented the spinning mule, a machine that combined the spinning jenny and the water frame.

1785 . . . .   Edmund Cartwright patented the first power loom.

1790 . . . .   Samuel Slater built the first water-powered machines in the U.S. for spinning cotton.

1793 . . . .   Eli Whitney invented the cotton gin. (See the illustration.)

1800 . . . .   Ireland exported 25 million yards of woven linen.

1804 . . . .   Jacquard loom used punched cards to enable a single weaver to produce complex patterned fabric. This is an early example of computer technology.

1816 . . . .   Power looms were beginning to be installed in large numbers in America.

1861 . . . .   Union soldiers wore uniforms that were machine-made. Confederate uniforms were still mostly made from handspun and handwoven fabric.

1884 . . . .   Hilaire Chardonnet developed the first manufactured fiber, a form of rayon.

1900s . . . .   The Industrial Revolution completed sweeping spinning and weaving from the home workshops to the factories and mills.

1910 . . . .   Chardonnet's fiber first produced in the U.S. under the name of artificial silk, now known as rayon.

1935 . . . .   Wallace H. Carrothers developed nylon.

1940s–1950s . . . . . .   Polyester, acrylic, and other artificial fibers were introduced.

1960s . . . .   Double-knit polyester fiber was introduced.

1970s . . . .   Knitting machines controlled by computers produced fabrics with highly complex patterns at tremendous speeds.

Early 1980s . . . . . .   Robots were introduced into the textile industry.

Late 1980s . . . .   Textile mills used high-speed looms that had many tiny shuttles called darts instead of a single shuttle. Other looms were used to weave with no shuttles at all. A jet of water or air carried the filling through the warp up to 1000 times a minute—four times faster than a shuttle on a standard high-speed loom.

TEN TOP EVENTS IN THE HISTORY OF TEXTILES

Look at your list of events that occurred as part of the history of textiles. Pick out the ten that you consider to be the most important. Write these in the spaces below.

1. _____
_____

2. _____
_____

3. _____
_____

4. _____
_____

5. _____
_____

6. _____
_____

7. _____
_____

8. _____
_____

9. _____
_____

10. _____
_____

After your class has constructed a class list of the Ten Top Events in the History of Textiles, use the back of this sheet to summarize the changes in society or the unmet needs society had that led to these developments.

■ THE CLOTHING INDUSTRY IN THE UNITED STATES THEN AND NOW

CONCEPTS

- Technological developments in the clothing industry were brought about by changes in society.
- Development of ready-to-wear garments was a technological revolution.
- The sewing machine transformed what people wore.
- The modern clothing industry democratized America.

OBJECTIVES

The student will:

- learn about social and technological developments in the clothing industry in America
- be introduced to the process of modern clothing production
- explore where modern clothing is produced for the United States
- identify the advantages and disadvantages of the current system of clothing production for the United States

TEACHER PREPARATION

- Prepare copies of the activity sheets "Clothing Production—Then and Now," "From Fabric to Garment," and "Pluses and Minuses."
- Check your knowledge of the history of clothing production and the steps taken in the production of most ready-to-wear garments. Some easy-to-find sources of basic information are listed under Background Information.
- Make a list of the countries where clothing sold in your local stores is produced.
- Be prepared to discuss the effects of foreign production on employment in the United States, the trade deficit, the cost of clothing for consumers; that is, the advantages and disadvantages of the current system of providing clothing to the consumer in the United States.

ACTIVITIES

1. Begin this lesson by asking students how what they wear today is different from what their ancestors wore. What brought these changes about? What made them possible? The task for today is to find out the answers to these and other questions related to how our clothing is, and has been, manufactured. Distribute the activity sheet "Clothing Production—Then and Now." Have students fill in the missing information as you discuss the history of clothing production in the United States. The intent here is not to conduct an in-depth review, but to show how societal changes and certain unmet needs led to the technological developments that revolutionized what we wear.

2. Summarize the discussion of the history of clothing production by showing how the following statements are true: (a) The development of the ready-to-wear garment was a technological revolution; (b) What people wore was transformed in a single generation; (c) The modern clothing industry democratized society in America.

3. Distribute the activity sheet "From Fabric to Garment." At the overhead projector, discuss and summarize the steps used to turn fabric into a finished ready-to-wear garment. Check the resource list and the list of production steps given under Background Information for ideas for this discussion.

4. Conclude this lesson by distributing the activity sheet "Pluses and Minuses." Ask the students to list advantages and disadvantages of the way America's clothing is manufactured. Refer to your notes about the effects of foreign production on the United States. It is important that students synthesize their thoughts so they realize the full impact of the pluses and minuses of how what they wear is being produced and how they are paying for it. Such issues as loss of jobs, lower prices, and the trade deficit should be discussed.

BACKGROUND INFORMATION

1. Some easy-to-find sources of information for this lesson are the following:
   "Clothing," *The Encyclopedia American International Edition* (1988), 7, 104–107.
   "Clothing," *The World Book Encyclopedia* (1986), 4, 536–557.
   "Clothing Industry," *Academic American Encyclopedia* (1985), 7, 65–66.
   "Industries, Textile," *The New Encyclopaedia Brittanica* (1987), Macropaedia 21, 508–526.
   "Textile Industry," *Academic American Encyclopedia* (1985), 19, 135–137.
   "Textiles," *The World Book Encyclopedia* (1986), 19, 168–173.

2. Here is a list of production steps from fabric to garment:
   a. Designer chooses fabric swatches.
   b. The design, a sketch, is completed.
   c. Final fabric and color are selected.
   d. A sample garment is made up.
   e. Cost sheet detailing expenditures for fabric, trimmings, findings, labor, and transportation is completed.
   f. Wholesale price is established.
   g. Production pattern is prepared and graded for sizes to be produced.
   h. Fabric is laid out in multiple layers and cut by machine.

   i. Cut goods are bundled and moved to sewing room.
   j. Assembly is completed, passing garment along an assembly line where each step is sewn.
   k. Final inspection is completed.
   l. Garments are pressed and packed or hung on racks.
   m. Finished garments are shipped to retailers.

CLOTHING PRODUCTION—THEN AND NOW

The production of ready-to-wear garments, often referred to as the (1) _____ _____, is a relatively recent development. Our modern method of (2) _____ production of clothing did not exist before the middle of the 1800's.

As you have seen from your study of textiles, there had been important advances to improve the (3) _____ of (4) _____ and (5) _____. After (6) _____ _____ were introduced in the Middle Ages, no new technology came upon the scene until 1851 when (7) _____ _____ designed a (8) _____ - _____ sewing machine. His machine was important because it freed the (9) _____ to hold and guide the material through the (10) _____. Other inventions were introduced. A (11) _____ _____ was developed that could cut through several (12) _____ of (13) _____ at a time. This machine has been replaced by one that uses (14) _____ to melt the cloth rather than cut it. A machine to automatically (15) _____ the fabric on the (16) _____ _____, a (17) _____ maker, a machine for sewing on (18) _____, and a (19) _____ machine that replaced the hand (20) _____ greatly improved the speed and accuracy of manufacturing ready-to-wear garments,

In the United States, the modern clothing industry probably started in (21) _____ in the early (22) _____. A very small "cottage" type industry was producing ready-to-wear clothing for (23) _____. They couldn't stay in port long enough to have (24) _____ made so they had been buying (25) _____ clothing. When the supply couldn't keep up with the (26) _____, this enterprise started.

Beginning in about 1825, men's (27) _____ began to stock easy-to-fit items like (28) _____, (29) _____, and so forth. By 1831, men's and boys' clothing production was starting in earnest in (30) _____, (31) _____, (32) _____, and (33) _____. The (34) _____ took place in shops set up for this purpose. The (35) _____ was completed by women and (36) _____ _____ and was still done by (37) _____.

When Singer's (38) _____ _____ became available in (39) _____, it (40) _____ the industry. One of these machines could stitch (41) _____ stitches a minute while a skilled seamstress could sew only (42) _____ a minute!

(continued)

CLOTHING PRODUCTION—THEN AND NOW (continued)

Slowly, the tailoring and dressmaking shops were made into small (43) _____. People bought several machines and trained others to use them. During this time period, a large number of (44) _____ settled in the large cities. They formed a large pool of labor available to assemble garments in their homes. During the (45) _____ century, much of the clothing produced was assembled by people, often whole families, in their tenement (46) _____. They took the bundles of cut pieces and (47) _____ them together at home.

The start of the (48) _____ _____ in 1861 brought about a tremendous demand for (49) _____. The old ways would no longer do. Manufacturers introduced the (50) _____ line. The (51) _____ needed to sew on the line were easily taught. (52) _____ sizes were developed from the measurements taken from several thousand soldiers. This idea soon carried over to all types of clothing.

By the 1880s, the (53) _____ _____ industry was established. The industrialization of clothing production for (54) _____ and (55) _____ progressed more slowly. Mass-produced (56) _____ and (57) _____ _____ were available in the middle to late 1800's. The Gibson Girl became very popular in the 1890's and mass-produced (58) _____ met the style demands of a whole generation.

By the beginning of the 20th century, clothing was being produced in factories in most cities. Thousands of (59) _____ filled the need for sewing machine operators. They worked in crowded shops in terrible conditions. These places were called (60) _____. They worked (61) _____ hours a day. A highly skilled person might earn (62) _____ per week while a beginner would earn only (63) _____.

On March 25, 1911, a fire at the (64) _____ _____ _____ in New York City resulted in the death of 146 people. This act and the abuses of the sweatshops brought much public attention to the working conditions. Large numbers of (65) _____ workers joined the unions. For years, the unions made slow progress in getting better (66) _____, (67) _____ _____, and (68) _____ _____. By the end of (69) _____ most workers were entitled to (70) _____ _____ and (71) _____ _____.

In the 1920's, a group of buildings were constructed on New York City's (72) _____ _____. They were built to house the (73) _____ and (74) _____ of the

CLOTHING PRODUCTION—THEN AND NOW (continued)

garment industry. Additional changes were made in the manufacturing process. What is known as (75) _____-_____ production was established. Each worker sewed only a (76) _____ _____ of the garment. This (77) _____ the length of time it took a person to get skillful. The worker was paid so much for each (78) _____ sewn correctly. This change speeded up production and lowered the cost of ready-to-wear apparel.

By 1930, American (79) _____ were being promoted by several large department stores. World War II cut America off from the fashion center in (80) _____. By 1950, Seventh Avenue was the heart of the women's fashion industry in America.

The past thirty years have seen radical changes in the United States (81) _____ industry. New York City remains the center of (82) _____ _____, but (83) _____ has moved elsewhere. Several of the well-known (84) _____ _____ no longer (85) _____ their line of clothing. They only (86) _____ and (87) _____ it. The actual production is done by other (88) _____ and (89) _____ companies.

The 1970's and 1980's saw (90) _____ technology begin to be used in the apparel industry. (91) _____ (Computer Assisted Design) systems were being used to produce designs and (92) _____. (93) _____ were doing the folding and cutting of fabric. Self-threading machines with (94) _____,_____ were making the sewing function easier.

Beginning in the (95) _____, some U.S. companies transferred their manufacturing processes (96) _____. They moved their whole operations to other (97) _____ where garments could be assembled at (98) _____ cost. (99) _____, (100) _____, (101) _____, and other Far Eastern and Eastern European countries are favorite locations for American manufacturers. More change to the industry was brought about by foreign countries importing vast amounts of clothing (102) _____, (103) _____, (104) _____, and (105) _____ are the largest (106) _____ of ready-to-wear apparel to the United States. Because these countries pay their workers so much (107) _____ than U.S. wages, their products tend to cost (108) _____. Although trade agreements have been (109) _____, these conditions continue to create severe problems for the U.S. clothing industry. By the middle of the (110) _____, the United States was (111) _____ almost (112) _____ times as much clothing as it was (113) _____!

FROM FABRIC TO GARMENT

There are many steps in the process to produce a ready-to-wear garment. You may be surprised to learn how many there are! Make a list of the steps involved in changing a piece of fabric to a ready-to-wear garment in the retailer's shop.

_____

_____

_____

_____

_____

_____

_____

_____

_____

_____

_____

_____

_____

_____

_____

_____

_____

_____

_____

_____

_____

_____

_____

PLUSES AND MINUSES

You have learned that the clothing industry has undergone many changes. Here in the last decade of the 20th century, the industry continues to have both advantages and disadvantages for the consumer. Make a list of them below.

Advantages	Disadvantages

© 1990 by The Center for Applied Research in Education

■ CONSUMERS DEMAND, INDUSTRY RESPONDS

CONCEPTS

- Industry has responded to consumers' demands that fabrics have certain characteristics.
- Consumers' demands led to the development of synthetic fibers.

OBJECTIVES

The student will:

- learn about the desirable characteristics consumers have demanded in fabrics
- learn the differences between natural, synthetic, and blended fabrics

TEACHER PREPARATION

- Check your knowledge of the characteristics of fabrics, of natural and man-made fibers, and the strengths and weaknesses of natural and synthetic fibers.
- You may want to consider sending for several publications to use in class. See Background Information.
- Make copies of the activity sheets "Characteristics of Fabrics," "A Guide to Fibers," and "Advantages and Disadvantages of Different Fibers."

ACTIVITIES

1. In this lesson, you will analyze the demands made by consumers that led to the development of synthetic fibers and certain finishing processes for fabrics made from natural fibers. Begin by describing some of the fabrics used by early settlers. Discuss linsey woolsey, for example. What was it? What was it used for? What did it look like? Feel like? Ask students how modern clothing differs. What are some of the characteristics of modern fabrics not found in linsey woolsey? Distribute the activity sheet "Characteristics of Fabrics." Discuss characteristics consumers have demanded that are listed on the activity sheet.

2. Point out that not all of these characteristics are possible in fabrics made with natural fibers. Discuss how industry responded by creating synthetic fibers from which fabrics could be made.

189

Ask students the names of synthetic fabrics. State that natural and synthetic fibers can be mixed to create a fabric we refer to as a blend. Review the characteristics of fabrics. Have students complete the activity sheet "A Guide to Fibers" as you conduct your discussion. Include such characteristics as durability, soil resistance, ease of ironing, strength, versatility, drying time, cost, shape retention, wrinkle resistance, insulating capacity, and so on. As a minimum, include cotton, linen, silk, wool, acetate, acrylic, nylon, polyester, and rayon. You may need to clarify that these fibers are used in fabrics that have many trade names. For example, Dacron™, Fortrel™, Kodel™, and Trevira™ are trade names for polyester fabrics.

3. For the last activity in this lesson, discuss the strengths and weaknesses of different fibers. Include in your list of fibers those you chose above. Have the students take notes about your discussion on the activity sheet "Advantages and Disadvantages of Different Fibers."

4. Conclude the lesson by pointing out how a knowledge of fibers and fabrics can be helpful in selecting clothing most appropriate for the environment in which it will be worn. Give several examples.

BACKGROUND INFORMATION

1. The American Fiber Manufacturers Association, Inc., provides some free and inexpensive materials that can be used in this lesson. (Prices and conditions are always subject to change, so check first with the Association before sending payment.) These materials are (a) *Manufactured Fiber Fact Book* ($5.00 per copy, 25% discount on ten copies or more); (b) *Guide to Man-Made Fibers* (free); (c) *Quick Guide to Manufactured Fibers* (free); (d) *Manufactured Fibers* video tape which gives detailed information on the history, manufacturing process, characteristics and end uses of manufactured fibers ($25.00 VHS, $30.00 3/4″ tape).

    To order, call or write the Education Department, American Fiber Manufacturers Association, Inc., 1150 17th Street NW, Suite 310, Washington, D.C. 20036, (202) 296-6508.

2. A large wall chart called "101 Durable Press, All Wool, Cotton, Blended, Funky Flannel, Wide Wale Textile Terms" is available from American Textile Manufacturers Institute, Inc., 400 South Tryon, Charlotte, NC 28285.

3. If you have access to a computer lab, you may want to consider using *Fiber Basic for Clothing*, a software program that lets students select fabrics such as cotton, wool, silk, nylon, polyester, acetate, rayon, acrylic, and spandex. The software teaches where these fabrics come from, the advantages and disadvantages of each, and their unique qualities. "Fiber Match Challenge" is a game included on the diskette. Order from: Career Aids, 20417 Nordhoff Street, Department EM3, Chatsworth, CA 91311. For the Apple, the program costs $49.00.

CHARACTERISTICS OF FABRICS

Consumers have demanded that the fabrics they use in the manufacture of clothing possess certain characteristics. The most common are listed in the chart below. Your job is to write a brief description of each characteristic in the space provided. (The illustration shows a spinneret.)

Characteristic	*Description*
Durability	
Permanent press	
Soil retardant	
Antistatic	
Water repellent	
Anti-shrinking	
Colorfast	
Soft	

Name _____   Date _____

A GUIDE TO FIBERS

Different fibers are used in different fabrics to give them certain characteristics. In the spaces below, list the common fabrics and their characteristics for the fibers shown. (The illustrations shows fiber filaments.)

Fiber	Common Fabrics	Characteristics
Cotton		
Linen		
Silk		
Wool		
Acetate		
Acrylic		
Nylon		
Polyester		
Rayon		

Name _____   Date _____

STRENGTHS AND WEAKNESSES
OF NATURAL AND SYNTHETIC FIBERS

Fabrics made from natural and synthetic fibers each have their own set of strengths and weaknesses. In the chart below, summarize the major strength and weakness for each fiber listed. (The illustration shows fabric weaves.)

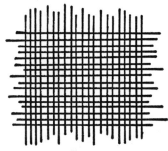

Fiber	*Strength*	*Weakness*
Cotton		
Linen		
Silk		
Wool		
Acetate		
Acrylic		
Nylon		
Polyester		
Rayon		

© 1990 by The Center for Applied Research in Education

■ SELECTION AND CARE OF FABRIC

CONCEPTS

- Different fabrics are more appropriate for different garments.
- Proper care extends the life of fabric.

OBJECTIVES

The students will:

- learn which fabrics are most appropriate for a selected list of garments
- become familiar with the steps involved in the proper care of fabrics

TEACHER PREPARATION

- Make copies of the activity sheets "What's Best for What?" and "How Do I Take Care of It?"
- Assemble a group of references (books, periodicals, pamphlets, and articles) about the type of fabric best suited for such garments as underwear, slacks, trousers, socks, blouses, shirts, jeans, suits, sweaters, jackets, raincoats, and so on.
- Collect a set of sample care labels from garments or prepare a set of cards that simulate care labels.
- You may want to conduct the first activity in a small group format. If so, decide on the composition of the small groups.

ACTIVITIES

1. Begin this lesson with a brief discussion of the importance of selecting garments made of an appropriate fabric. Give several concrete examples of both appropriate and inappropriate choices. Distribute the activity sheet "What's Best for What?" and review the assignment. Be sure to provide students with the list of garments they are to research. Point out that they may need to refer to the information about fibers they learned in previous lessons. If you are having the students work in small groups, review any working rules you may have established for this type of activity. Circulate around the room and help those students who may be experiencing difficulty.

Another option is to simply conduct a class discussion of what fabrics to choose for a selected list of garments and have the students fill in the information on the activity sheet.

2. When the students have finished this task, have individual students or a group share their findings. You should solidify the importance of selecting garments made from fabrics with characteristics most appropriate for the intended use of the garment.

3. The final activity for this lesson is to present information about how to care for the fabrics and to outline the reasons for proper care. Begin the investigation of this topic by passing around samples of care labels or the cards you prepared to simulate care labels. Ask students to identify the cards. Ask several students to read what their cards say. Ask if they noticed that not all labels say the same thing. Why is this? Different fabrics require different care. Why should we be concerned about caring for fabrics properly? What are the benefits of proper care? What different functions are included in proper care? Do we only need to be concerned about washing or dry cleaning? Why not? Select a fabric and ask the students how to take care of it for washing, drying, and ironing. Have the students use the information on the care labels or cards to try and provide you with the information. When students realize that there is more to the proper care of fabrics than meets the eye, distribute the activity sheet "How Do I Take Care of It?" Have the students complete the activity sheet as you explain what each label statement means.

4. Conclude the lesson by discussing what can happen to fabrics if they are not cared for properly.

WHAT'S BEST FOR WHAT?

Today, you are going to research which fabrics are most appropriate for a list of garments your teacher will give you. Write the name of the garment in the left-hand column. Be sure you give a reason for your fabric selection. You may need to refer to your notes from previous lessons.

Garment	Type of Fabric	Why?

Name _____   Date _____

HOW DO I TAKE CARE OF IT?

Knowing what the care label on a garment means is being a smart consumer! Today, you are going to learn information that could save you lots of money in the future.

If the Label Says This:	It Means This:
Machine Wash	
Home Launder Only	
No Bleach	
Cold Wash/Cold Rinse	
Warm Wash/Warm Rinse	
No Spin	
Hand Wash	
Wash Separately	
Delicate/Gentle Cycle	
Tumble Dry	
Tumble Dry/Remove Prompt	
Drip Dry	

(continued)

HOW DO I TAKE CARE OF IT? (continued)

Line Dry	
No Wring/Twist	
Dry Flat	
Block to Dry	
Cool Iron	
Warm Iron	
Hot Iron	
Do Not Iron	
Steam Iron	
Iron Damp	
Dry Clean Only	
Professional Dry Clean	
No Dry Clean	

■ CLOTHING EVALUATION

CONCEPTS

- Recognizing quality workmanship in articles of clothing can give you a shopping edge.
- The general appearance of a garment influences the decision to purchase or not.

OBJECTIVES

The student will:

- learn the points to consider when evaluating an article of clothing for quality of construction
- examine the individual features of a garment to determine the quality of construction and workmanship
- judge the overall quality of "off the rack" clothing to determine if it is a wise purchase

TEACHER PREPARATION

- Make copies of the activity sheets "Points to Consider" and "A Question of Quality."
- Examine both options given for the first activity and make a determination of which you will use.
- Check your knowledge of evaluating clothing and prepare a set of notes for the discussion called for in the first activity if Option 1 is selected, or select a filmstrip or video cassette that presents the information called for in "Points to Consider" if you use Option 2.
- Collect a set of articles of clothing for students to use to evaluate their quality. You might want to include such articles as a blouse, shirt, skirt, jeans, jacket, coat, suit, and trousers. The articles you select should contain an example of all of the items in "Points to Consider." Often, stores will loan a school garments for this purpose. Another option is to bring in personal items and ask student volunteers to bring in items. The articles should represent different price ranges.
- Organize the class into evaluation groups.

ACTIVITIES

1. Ask students if they can recognize quality clothing construction. What makes it different from shoddy construction? What characterizes good workmanship? Is workmanship the only thing to consider before selecting a garment? If not, what else is? Tell students that in this lesson they

will learn a set of criteria they can apply in the clothing selection process that will enable them to be better consumers. Distribute the activity sheet "Points to Consider."

Option 1

Discuss each point to consider from the activity sheet. Have students make notes in the spaces provided. Illustrate your discussion with examples from real garments, if at all possible. Provide students with the opportunity to see at close hand what you are talking about.

Option 2

Show the filmstrip or video of "Clothing: A Consumer's Guide" (see Background Information). This presentation discusses the information contained in "Points to Consider." In addition, it presents information about textiles and where to shop.

2. Now that students know some of the features to look for when evaluating a garment, tell them they are going to be put to the test! How well can they select quality clothing? Distribute the activity sheet "A Question of Quality" and review the assignment. Assign students to groups, point out that they should select a reporter who will report the group's findings, and clarify any questions they may have. Remind students that they should treat the garments with care because they have been borrowed and must be returned in good condition. Distribute an article to each group and let the groups get to work.

3. When the groups have completed their evaluation, have a reporter from each group display the article of clothing and discuss each feature that was evaluated. The reporter should give the group's overall decision regarding whether or not to purchase the article with an explanation of the reasons for the decision.

4. Bring the lesson to a close by having the students summarize what to look for in garments being considered for purchase. Be sure to include materials, construction techniques, and workmanship.

BACKGROUND INFORMATION

The filmstrip "Clothing: A Consumer's Guide" may be purchased from Learning Seed, 330 Tester Road, Lake Zurich, IL 60047. The filmstrip and cassette cost $69.00; the video cassette, $79.00.

POINTS TO CONSIDER

There are some important things to look for when you examine a garment with an eye toward purchasing it. Your teacher will tell you about the things to look for, and show you examples in real garments. Remember, this is no exercise! Knowing what to look for in quality construction, workmanship, and materials will save you money!

In the space provided, jot down the important facts to remember about each ''point to consider.''

1. FABRIC _____

_____

2. GRAINLINE _____

_____

3. PLAIDS, CHECKS, STRIPES _____

_____

4. FABRIC WITH PILE OR NAP _____

_____

5. INTERFACING, LINING, UNDERLINING _____

_____

6. TOP-STITCHING _____

_____

7. DARTS _____

_____

8. GATHERING _____

_____

9. SEAMS _____

_____

10. COLLARS _____

_____

(continued)

POINTS TO CONSIDER (continued)

11. SET-IN SLEEVES _____

_____

12. HEMS _____

_____

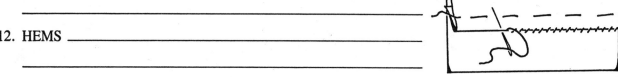

13. PLACKETS _____

_____

14. ZIPPERS _____

_____

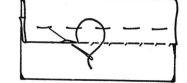

15. BUTTONHOLES _____

_____

16. BUTTONS _____

_____

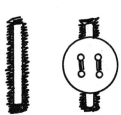

17. BELTS, WAISTBANDS _____

_____

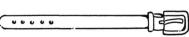

18. PRESSING _____

_____

A QUESTION OF QUALITY

You and a group of your classmates will be given an article of clothing to evaluate. Use the information from "Points to Consider" to help you answer the questions below. Be thorough in your examination, but remember to treat the garment with care because it has been borrowed. Appoint a reporter for your group to report your findings to the class.

GARMENT: _____

Directions: Check the appropriate box for each item in the chart below. (NA means "not applicable.")

FABRIC

	Yes	No	NA
Are plaids, stripes, large prints matched at the seams?			
Is the fabric suitable for the garment?			
Is it cut on the grainline?			
Is the nap or pile cut in one direction?			

LINING AND INTERFACING

Are they smooth and the correct weight for the garment?			

STITCHING

Is the top-stitching straight?			
Is the thread the correct color?			
Is the stitching secure in all places?			

DARTS

Are they symmetrical?			
Are they smooth and well secured at the ends?			

SEAMS

Are they set in smoothly, without puckers or gathers?			
Are they stitched (if necessary)?			

(continued)

A QUESTION OF QUALITY (continued)

COLLAR

	Yes	No	NA
Does it lie smooth?			
Are the points the same distance apart?			

SLEEVES

Are they set in smoothly, without puckers or gathers? . . . .

HEM

Is it smooth, almost invisible, and an even width? . . . .

FASTENERS

Are they sewn on securely? . . . .

Are the buttonholes strong? . . . .

Does the zipper work easily? . . . .

PRESSING

Is it free from wrinkles? . . . .

Are there pulls or snags? . . . .

WAISTBANDS

Is it firm? . . . .

Does it roll? . . . .

Does the overlap of the waistband finish flush with the placket? . . . .

Is the overall appearance of the garment pleasing to the eye? YES _____ NO _____

Should this article of clothing be considered for purchase? YES _____ NO _____

Why? _____

_____

_____

_____

■ COLOR AND YOU

CONCEPTS

- Color selection influences how well you look in clothes.

OBJECTIVES

The student will:

- learn about color theory
- discuss the elements of color theory as they apply to clothing selection
- determine whether cool colors (blue/green) or warm colors (orange/yellow) enhance his or her skin, eye, and hair color
- apply color theory to wardrobe planning

TEACHER PREPARATION

- Read *Color Me Beautiful* by Carole Jackson or *New Images for Women* by Gerrie Pinchkey and Marge Swenson. These will strengthen your knowledge of color theory and its application to wardrobe planning and enhancement of personal appearance. Be sure to remember that color theory is just as applicable to men as it is to women!
- Obtain a color swatch kit that has colors coded by seasons. You will need this to help students determine their color season.
- Obtain a color palette to go with the swatch kit. You can go to a local paint store and select color samples for each of the seasons to make up your own palette.
- Have pieces of gold and silver jewelry for demonstration purposes.
- Make copies of the activity sheets "Color and You" and "Color Theory."
- If your classroom is not equipped with several large mirrors, you may want to consider moving to the sewing room.
- Make a selection among Options 1, 2, and 3 to use in the second activity.

ACTIVITIES

1. Ask the students if they have a favorite color. When they select clothing, do they often buy garments in their favorite color? Do people tell them they look nice when they wear certain colors? Point out that people look their best when they wear styles and fabric designs that are best for their figure type and in colors that complement their skin, eye, and hair color. The purpose of this lesson is to show them how they can make colors work for them.

2. Distribute the activity sheet "Color Theory" and briefly discuss Munsell's Color system that is based on the five primary colors: red, yellow, green, blue, and purple. Define the terms given on the activity sheet, and have the students write the definitions in the spaces provided. Describe the four color seasons and their characteristics. Explain how a person determines his or her season.

Option 1

Distribute the activity sheet "Color and You." Have the students predict their color season. Select a student to use as a model, drape him or her with samples from the swatch kit, and determine his or her color season. You should demonstrate the process you want the students to use to complete this activity. That process is as follows:

a. Examine hair, skin, and eye color.
b. Determine whether the person has blue undertones or yellow to narrow the choice to winter/ summer or spring/autumn.
c. Use fabric swatches for cool and warm tones when draping the student to help identify the correct season. Hold the silver and gold jewelry near the hair. The one that complements rather than clashes with the hair color helps determine whether the person tends toward warm or cool colors.
d. Decide which colors of the two seasons within the cool or warm range look best on the individual.

Option 2

"Color Cues" is a filmstrip that can be used to demonstrate the process of determining one's color season. The filmstrip shows a person from each of the four seasons, discusses why certain colors enhance or detract from the person's skin, hair, and eye color, and gives an interesting presentation of the theory of color. Fabric swatches come with the filmstrip. This kit may be ordered for $69.00 from Color Cues, P.O. Box 401474, Dallas, TX 75240.

Option 3

Invite a color consultant to class as a guest speaker to achieve the objectives outlined in this lesson.

3. Ask the students to select a partner. If you do not have enough swatches and palettes, you may have to work in groups. Explain to the students that they will go through the process you just outlined to determine their color season. Distribute the necessary materials and have students gather around a mirror, if possible. Assist the students as they attempt this task.

4. When they have determined their color seasons, hold a general discussion about the process they used. Allow time for some to complain about colors on their palette that they do not like. Explain

that this is personality. We all have likes and dislikes. Show students a color palette that can be purchased from a color consultant. Explain the use of the color palette. Show students how to use it to select garments that will enhance appearance. Discuss how the use of the palette simplifies shopping. Explain the statement, "If it isn't in your color range, it will decorate your closet, not you!"

5. Conclude the lesson by having students brainstorm how knowledge of one's color season can be a help in shopping for clothes. Summarize how a smart consumer uses a color palette to make decisions about clothing selection.

COLOR THEORY

Your teacher will be presenting some interesting information about colors and their effect on appearance. To get started, listen closely and write the answers to the following questions in the spaces provided.

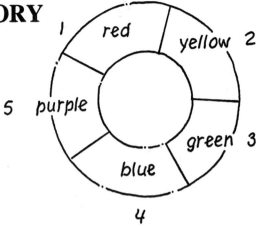

1. What are the five primary colors in Munsell's Color

System? _____

_____

_____

2. Munsell defined color by measured scales of hue, value, and chroma.

   a. What is hue? _____

_____

   b. What is color value? _____

_____

   c. What is chroma? _____

_____

   d. What is undertone? _____

_____

   e. What is pigment? _____

_____

   f. What is melanin? _____

_____

3. What are the four color seasons? _____

4. What determines an individual's season? _____

_____

(continued)

COLOR THEORY (continued)

5. People who are classified as winter or summer are considered to have _____ under-tones.

6. People who are classified as spring or autumn are considered to have _____ under-tones.

7. List the skin, hair, and eye color most commonly associated with each season:

   a. Winter _____

   _____

   _____

   b. Summer _____

   _____

   _____

   c. Spring _____

   _____

   _____

   d. Autumn _____

   _____

   _____

Name _____ Date _____

COLOR AND YOU

Now it is your turn. You and a partner or a group of classmates will determine your color season and their color season. Remember, there is an organized process to do this. Here are the steps:

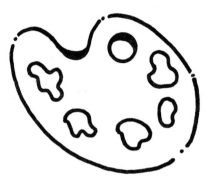

1. Examine hair, skin, and eye color.
2. Determine whether the person has blue undertones or yellow undertones to narrow the choice to winter/summer or spring/autumn.
3. Drape cool- and warm-colored fabric swatches on the person to help you identify the correct season. Hold gold and silver jewelry near the person's hair to see if it complements or clashes with the hair color. The one that complements helps determine whether the person tends toward warm or cool colors.
4. Decide which colors of the two seasons within the cool or warm range look best on the individual.

1. I predict my color season is _____ because I _____
_____
_____

2. According to my partner(s), my skin undertone is _____; therefore, I am either
_____ or _____.

3. After being draped with the color swatches, it appears that my group believes my season is
_____.

4. I agree/do not agree with my group's decision. (Circle the correct answer.) Why? _____
_____
_____

5. I should buy clothes in the following colors: _____
_____
_____

6. A neutral color is _____. Why is it important in wardrobe planning? _____
_____
_____

7. How are most bright colors used when coordinating an outfit? _____
_____
_____

8. I will be able to select garments in my colors when I go shopping by _____
_____
_____

■ PLANNING A WARDROBE

CONCEPTS

- Knowledge of design principles and design elements helps an individual make wise clothing decisions.

OBJECTIVES

The student will:

- learn the elements of clothing design
- learn clothing design principles
- practice identifying specific principles and elements of design
- apply the elements and principles of design to select articles of clothing
- select articles of clothing for specific body types

TEACHER PREPARATION

- Make copies of the activity sheets "Line and Design" and "Wardrobe—A Blueprint for Success!"
- Prepare information for a discussion about selecting clothing for a wardrobe. Such topics as the following should be included: principles of clothing design (proportion, balance, rhythm, and emphasis), and the elements of clothing design (line, color, and texture).
- Collect fashion magazines and catalogs for students to use in class.
- Collect examples of clothing or pictures of clothes that illustrate design principles.
- Collect pictures of gardens, table settings, wrapped gifts, bulletin board ideas, well-designed buildings or homes, and garnished foods.

ACTIVITIES

1. Begin this lesson by showing students pictures of a nicely set table, a beautifully wrapped gift, a well-laid-out flower or vegetable garden, a house or building, and food that is nicely displayed or garnished. Ask the students if the pictures have visual appeal. How do they do that? What makes the pictures attractive? Could the same elements of attractiveness be applied to wardrobe planning? Distribute the activity sheet "Line and Design." Briefly explain the procedure for

students to complete the activity sheet as you discuss wardrobes as related to principles and elements of clothing design. Use photo examples and actual articles of clothing to illustrate each principle and/or element. Explain how the elements and principles can work to improve the appearance of body proportions, accent such traits as hair and eye color and complexion, and improve personal image. Include information to consider before adding items to your wardrobe. Conclude this activity by having students verbally summarize the elements and principles of design. Ask if they have universal application. In what way? Show the pictures used at the beginning of this activity, and have the students identify a design element or principle present in the photo.

2. Distribute fashion magazines, catalogs, and the activity sheet "Wardrobe—A Blueprint for Success." Explain that they will practice selecting clothing based on their new-found knowledge about design elements and principles. Have students work alone or in small groups to determine appropriate styles of clothing for each person described on the activity sheet. Remind them to support their selections with facts about design.

3. When students have completed this task, review their findings with the class. Have the class verify each selection and reason(s) for same.

4. Bring this lesson to a close by asking students to describe a process they could use to identify items of clothing for their own wardrobe. You could set the stage with a scenario. You are about to go shopping for a new _____ (season) wardrobe at _____ (a local store). What process will you use to select clothing that will most enhance your appearance?

BACKGROUND INFORMATION

This lesson lends itself to a number of interesting extensions. You could, for example, have a fashion consultant conduct this lesson. You could videotape selected clips from popular TV shows and have the students evaluate what the actors and actresses are wearing. You could have a local store present a mini-fashion show to show appropriate and inappropriate selections for particular individuals.

LINE AND DESIGN

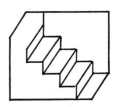

Your teacher will be discussing some very important information about what makes a person look nice in clothes. What is there about the design of clothes that makes them appropriate for some people and not for others?

Listen carefully and complete the following questions. If you can learn this information and know how to apply it, you are on your way to having your name placed on the list of "Best Dressed Persons in America"!

© 1990 by The Center for Applied Research in Education

1. What is a wardrobe? _____

_____

2. What factors should be considered to determine an adequate wardrobe? _____

_____

_____

3. What is a design principle? _____

_____

_____

4. What are the principles of clothing design? _____

_____

_____

5. List some important facts to remember about each principle of clothing design. _____

_____

_____

_____

_____

_____

(continued)

LINE AND DESIGN (continued)

6. What are the elements of clothing design? _____

_____

_____

7. What can these elements, if used correctly, do for you? _____

_____

_____

_____

8. Before you purchase your wardrobe, you should consider the following:

_____

_____

_____

_____

_____

_____

_____

_____

_____

_____

_____

WARDROBE—A BLUEPRINT FOR SUCCESS!

Read the following body descriptions. Use your knowledge of design elements and principles to select appropriate clothing for each person described. Use the magazines and catalogs to find your selections. Mark the page of the magazine or catalog so that you can find it to show the class later. Be sure you are able to support your choices; state the reasons for making the selections you did.

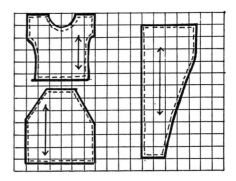

1. Sarah is petite. She has small stature and good proportion.

   a. Clothing selected: _____

   _____

   b. These items were selected because they included the following design elements and principles:

   _____

   _____

2. Vera is short and chubby.

   a. Clothing selected: _____

   _____

   b. These items were selected because they included the following design elements and principles:

   _____

   _____

3. Joe is tall and slender. He started growing in junior high and continues to get taller.

   a. Clothing selected: _____

   _____

   b. These items were selected because they included the following design elements and principles:

   _____

   _____

4. Bill is tall, but slightly overweight.

   a. Clothing selected: _____

   _____

   b. These items were selected because they included the following design elements and principles:

   _____

   _____

WARDROBE—A BLUEPRINT FOR SUCCESS! (continued)

5. Laura is average height, but her hips are large in proportion to her total body size.

  a. Clothing selected: _____

  _____

  b. These items were selected because they included the following design elements and principles:

  _____

  _____

6. Jack is "long waisted," that is, long between the neck and waist in relation to other measurements. He is the correct weight for his height.

  a. Clothing selected: _____

  _____

  b. These items were selected because they included the following design elements and principles:

  _____

  _____

7. Susan is "short waisted," that is, short between the neck and waist in relation to other measurements. She is the correct weight for her height.

  a. Clothing selected: _____

  _____

  b. These items were selected because they included the following design elements and principles:

  _____

  _____

8. Analyze your own body proportions. Find illustrations of clothing that show good line, texture, and color for you. Why are these items of clothing a good choice for you in terms of design principles?

  _____

  _____

  _____

  _____

  _____

  _____

  _____

  _____

  _____

  _____

■ SEWING MACHINES—THE OLD AND THE NEW

CONCEPTS

- Sewing machines are made up of a series of parts that each have a specific function.
- Sewing machines changed little until computer technology was applied to several functions.
- Sewing machines using computer technology can automatically complete processes unheard of a few years ago.
- The "right" sewing machine for you depends upon what you intend to do with it.

OBJECTIVES

The student will:

- be able to identify the parts of both a conventional and a high-technology sewing machine and describe their function
- learn about the technological advances in sewing machines
- list the advantages and disadvantages of conventional and computerized home sewing machines

TEACHER PREPARATION

- Make copies of the activity sheets "The Conventional Sewing Machine," "The Principle Parts," "The Computerized Sewing Machine," and "Comparing the Features."
- If you do not have a computerized sewing machine in your school or you cannot borrow one from a friend or a local dealer, locate pictures of computerized machines. Your local sewing machine dealer will have advertising brochures, may have large wall charts, and would probably be quite willing to conduct a demonstration in your classroom.
- Have a sewing machine available from your school's laboratory. If you have one of the new technology machines in your school, have it available also.

ACTIVITIES

1. During this lesson, students will learn about both conventional and high-technology sewing machines. If your school is equipped with the new computerized sewing machines, you may want to change the order of the activities. Explain that for most schools, conventional machines are used by

students in sewing classes because the new high-technology machines are still quite expensive. Show them a conventional machine. Distribute the activity sheet "The Conventional Sewing Machine" and have them read the introductory material. After they have completed reading the material, discuss each part of the conventional machine. Show students what it is, where it is located, and what it does. Have the students complete labeling the diagram.

2. Distribute the activity sheet "The Principle Parts" and the manuals for the sewing machines they will be using in later lessons to complete a sewing project. Have them use the manual as a resource to complete the activity sheet.

3. Bring this part of the lesson to a close by having students turn their activity sheets over or put them away. Then point to the various parts on your demonstration machine and ask students for the parts' names or give the name of a part and ask a student to point it out on the machine. You should also be checking to see if they know what each part does. This quick review will reinforce the students' knowledge of the conventional machine.

4. You are now ready to make a transition to the new technology. Ask students if they know anything about the functions of a microcomputer. For example, what is input, output, data retrieval, and so on? Where has computer technology been used in the home? What are some examples? What exactly does computer technology make possible? What are some advanced functions in home appliances made possible by computer technology? Could any of these have application to a sewing machine? Which ones?

   Distribute the activity sheet "The Computerized Sewing Machine." Have the students study the information presented. If you have a machine, point out and discuss the parts and functions that make it different from a conventional machine. If you do not have a machine, distribute brochures or use wall charts to discuss the differences. Be sure to discuss the processes (functions) possible on the new technology machines that are not possible on the conventional machine. In other words, what will a high-technology machine do that a conventional one will not? Also discuss the circumstances under which a conventional machine will do the job quite satisfactorily. What sewing jobs can a conventional machine do just as well as a high-technology machine? Have the students complete labeling the parts as illustrated. If time permits, you may want to conduct a quick review such as the one you did for the conventional machine in Activity 3.

5. It is important that students recognize that, just as in so many other consumer situations, it is important to know the advantages and disadvantages of conventional and high-technology sewing machines. If the consumer doesn't have this information and a clear picture of what he or she wants to do with a sewing machine, he or she may buy the wrong machine. The machine may be too conventional and not be able to sew fancy designs from memory, duplicate button holes one time after another, and so on. Or, the machine may do all of these things when all the consumer wants to do is mend and construct simple garments.

   Distribute the activity sheet "Comparing the Features." Have the students list the advantages and disadvantages as you discuss them. Bring the lesson to a close by once again reinforcing that the machine a person needs depends on a clear understanding of what it is to be used for. Both conventional and high-technology machines have their places. A good consumer selects only enough technology to get the job done that he or she wants done, not the job described by a fancy advertising brochure. America's closets are filled with the latest technological marvels that, too often, nobody uses!

THE CONVENTIONAL SEWING MACHINE

Sewing machines have been used in the home for well over a hundred years. You may remember that Isaac Singer designed the first treadle-powered machine in 1851. Sewing machines have changed little since that time. Of course, they were electrified; the tension controls improved; bobbins worked better; stitch length was more uniform—but they were basically the same machine.

These machines have been fine for their purpose. Millions of people have sewn their own clothing, made home furnishings such as draperies and slipcovers, made untold numbers of craft items, and performed the household mending. The conventional machine has served people well.

Conventional machines that are well made can be used for many years. They are what we call "cost effective." They are cost effective because they don't cost a lot to begin with, they don't require a lot of maintenance, and they go on working for thousands of hours.

Conventional machines come with a set of attachments that enable the user to do more complicated processes much easier. Constructing buttonholes is an example. These attachments almost always represent an extra cost.

You may be using a conventional machine later in this course. It is important that you know something about the parts and how they operate.

Watch closely as your teacher points out and demonstrates the parts of the demonstration machine. Label the diagram below with the name of the parts shown.

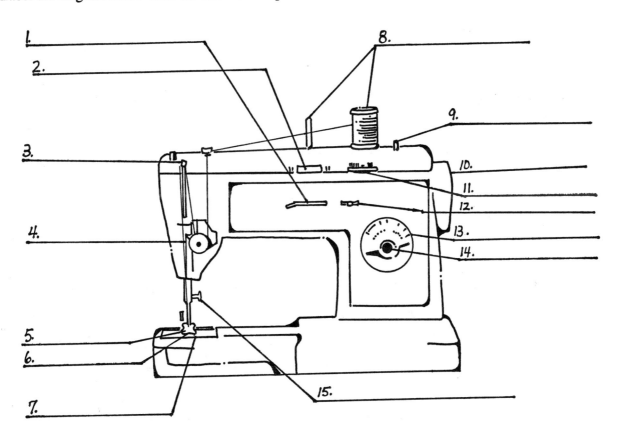

1. _____
2. _____
3. _____
4. _____
5. _____
6. _____
7. _____
8. _____
9. _____
10. _____
11. _____
12. _____
13. _____
14. _____
15. _____

THE PRINCIPLE PARTS

You have already learned something about the parts of a conventional sewing machine. Now use your sewing machine manual to write a definition of the parts listed below. Your definition should include a description of what the part does.

1. stitch control dial (length): _____

_____

2. presser foot: _____

_____

3. take-up level: _____

_____

4. tension dial: _____

_____

5. throat plate: _____

_____

6. hand wheel: _____

_____

7. needle position dial: _____

_____

8. reverse stitch lever: _____

_____

(continued)

THE PRINCIPLE PARTS (continued)

9. spool pin: _____
_____

10. stitch width dial: _____
_____

11. power and light switch: _____
_____

12. bobbin winder: _____
_____

13. needle clamp: _____
_____

14. presser foot lever: _____
_____

15. slide plate: _____
_____

16. foot control: _____
_____

17. feed: _____
_____

18. tension disc: _____
_____

THE COMPUTERIZED SEWING MACHINE

Advances in computer technology have been applied to the sewing machine. State-of-the-art machines provide speed and convenience along with the ability to scan, store, and retrieve data to complete complex functions. For instance, buttonhole memory matches all buttonholes to the length of the first one made. Many machines have programmable pattern designs, a needle-stop feature that cycles the needle up when the machine stops, and an automatic finishing stitch to secure seams at the beginning and end with extra stitches.

Some companies offer updated memory cassettes that provide an almost unlimited choice of stitches. One machine has an embroidery unit attachment that monograms as well as doing motifs.

Other computerized machines have a function called "sewing advisors." By entering information into a computer-like keyboard about the type of fabric and task to be completed, the machine automatically determines the best stitch type, length, and width as well as the appropriate presser foot and tension. This takes all of the guesswork out of sewing! This type of machine is a "smart" machine.

These machines can be very expensive. In 1989, the top-of-the-line models retailed for about $2400.

A diagram of a high-technology sewing machine is shown below. Note some obvious visual differences from a conventional machine. As your teacher demonstrates and discusses this type of machine, label the parts shown. The key words you will need to listen for are listed after the diagram.

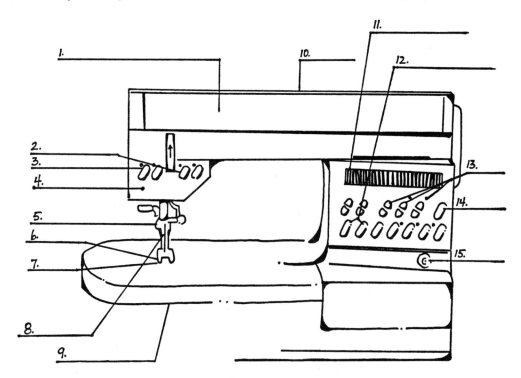

spool pin
automatic tie off
display key
reverse stitching
chart of preprogrammed
   stitches

digital display
dual feed
memory (storage)
automatic buttonhole
electronic bobbin thread
   monitor

needle position
presser foot
flatbed/free arm
automatic needle threader

222   (continued)

THE COMPUTERIZED SEWING MACHINE (continued)

QUESTIONS TO ANSWER

1. How do the conventional and computerized sewing machines differ visually? _____

_____

_____

_____

2. How do these machines differ functionally? _____

_____

_____

_____

3. Under what circumstances would you buy a high-technology home sewing machine? _____

_____

_____

_____

4. Describe the type of sewing rasks that would lead you to decide to purchase a conventional-type home sewing machine. _____

_____

_____

_____

_____

_____

COMPARING THE FEATURES

You have had a chance to discuss both the conventional and the new high-technology home sewing machines. If you were faced with a decision to select a sewing machine today, would you know which to choose? Remember one of the "Golden Rules of Home Economics": Good consumers ALWAYS do their research. They check out the advantages and disadvantages of a product before they make a decision.

During the next few minutes, you will be talking about the advantages and disadvantages of different types of sewing machines. List these advantages and disadvantages in the chart below.

	Conventional Machine	*High-Technology Machine*
Advantages		
Disadvantages		

■ GAINING CONTROL

CONCEPTS

- There is a specific set of procedures that lead to sewing proficiency.
- Knowledge of how to regulate the speed and guide the fabric over a designated path is essential to proficient sewing-machine operation.

OBJECTIVES

The students will:

- observe a demonstration of the operational procedures for a sewing machine
- observe a demonstration of how to control the speed of a sewing machine and guide the machine over a designated path
- practice using a sewing machine

TEACHER PREPARATION

- Set up a demonstration area.
- Make copies of the activity sheet "Gaining Control," which includes several stitching sheet patterns.

ACTIVITIES

1. Introduce the lesson by telling students they must learn to "control" the sewing machine if they are to complete a sewing project. Gaining control of the sewing machine takes knowledge and practice of the preliminary steps for operating a machine that should be followed each time you sew. Explain that they are going to practice using the sewing machine with paper stitching sheets.
2. Direct the students to the demonstration area. Show them how to position the paper, insert the needle, lower the presser foot, turn on the power, and use the foot control. Demonstrate guiding the needle over the lines on the paper.
3. Distribute the activity sheet "Gaining Control." Review the directions. Allow time for the students to practice.

4. Discuss how the parts of a sewing machine, like any other machine, work together. Ask the students if they felt they were in control of the machine. What techniques did they use to stay on the line? How did they control the speed of the machine? Has their confidence level increased?

5. Conclude this lesson by having the class list the steps to follow to maintain control over a sewing machine. Use the chalkboard or an overhead projector to focus student attention on this task. You may want to have students write the list in the "Notes" section of the activity sheet "Gaining Control."

Name _____ Date _____

GAINING CONTROL

You probably thought you'd never get your hands on a sewing machine! Well, now is your chance to demonstrate your talent. Read the directions carefully and complete each stitching pattern. Remember, you are trying to gain control over a machine. This is not a race. Try your best to keep your stitches on the lines. Good luck!

DIRECTIONS: Place the right side of the paper on the seam guideline. Insert the needle on the first line. Put the presser foot down. Turn on the sewing machine. Place your foot on the power control to start the machine. There should be no thread in the machine! Practice guiding the paper and controlling the speed while stitching on the line. Do the stitching sheets in order. Then give your best example to your teacher to check your progress.

NOTES

_____
_____
_____
_____
_____
_____
_____
_____
_____
_____
_____
_____
_____
_____
_____
_____
_____
_____
_____
_____

GAINING CONTROL: STITCHING PATTERN 1

GAINING CONTROL: STITCHING PATTERN 2

GAINING CONTROL: STITCHING PATTERN 3

Name _____ Date _____

GAINING CONTROL: STITCHING PATTERN 4

Find out what the word below is by connecting the dots in order as you stitch with the sewing machine.

■ READING THE PATTERN

CONCEPTS

- The successful use of a sewing pattern requires knowledge of a special vocabulary.
- There are marks on a pattern that specify certain actions to be taken in marking, cutting, and sewing fabric.

OBJECTIVES

The student will:

- learn the meaning of the symbols used on sewing patterns
- label a pattern diagram and identify the construction markings
- complete a crossword puzzle about pattern symbols and markings

TEACHER PREPARATION

- Prepare an overhead transparency of the activity sheet "Reading the Pattern."
- Make copies of the activity sheets "Reading the Pattern" and "Pattern Markings."

ACTIVITIES

1. Introduce the lesson by discussing the information on the activity sheet "Reading the Pattern." Use the overhead transparency of the activity sheet. Name each symbol and give a brief explanation of its use in marking, cutting, and sewing the fabric. Have the students complete their activity sheets as you discuss the information.
2. Have the students complete the crossword puzzle "Pattern Markings."
3. Next, direct the students to circle the markings on the pattern they will be using to complete their sewing project.
4. Conclude this lesson by showing students the bodice pattern piece and have them name each mark as you point to it. Remind students that they will need to use the markings properly if they are to be successful in completing their project.

READING THE PATTERN

Symbols found on a pattern are used to assist in the marking, cutting, and sewing of the fabric. If you are to be successful in sewing, you need to become familiar with the symbols and their meanings. Look at the diagram of the pattern piece below. Label the construction markings as your teacher lists them on the overhead transparency.

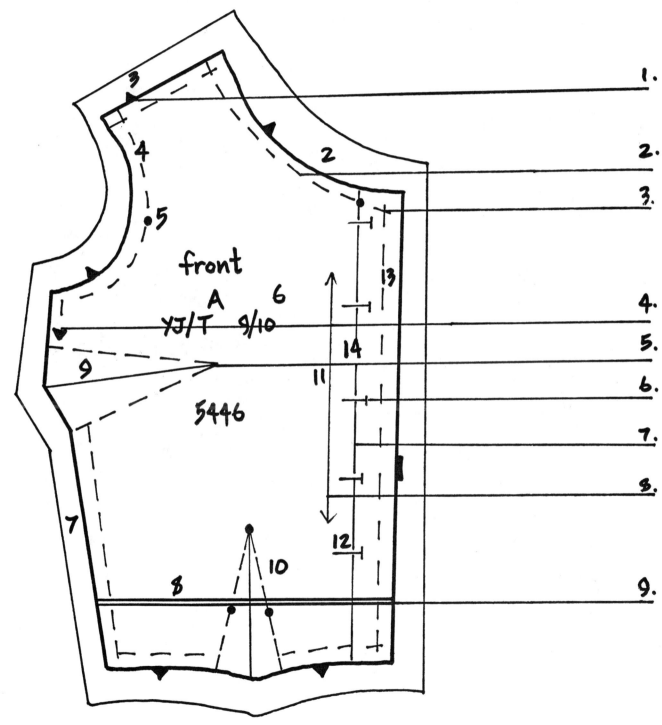

1.
2.
3.
4.
5.
6.
7.
8.
9.

PATTERN MARKINGS

ACROSS

2. Broken line to indicate where to let out; ease
7. Broken line to indicate where to take in
8. Alternating solid/broken line
9. Aids for matching seams
10. V-shaped symbols aid joining pattern pieces
12. Notations on pattern giving directions on what to do
13. Solid line having short line at right angle with one end when horizontal, two ends when vertical

DOWN

1. Short arrow indicating where to clip into the seam allowance to release it
3. On seamline to show direction in which pieces should be stitched
4. Arrowhead symbols with instructions for placing pattern on grain
5. Markings that serve as guideposts for putting together and sewing garment
6. Indicated by broken line ⅝″ from cutting line
8. Tissue paper guide for making a garment
9. Indicated by two broken lines for stitching, solid line at center for folding
11. Indicate center fold lines, some hemlines (2 words, no space between)

■ SAMPLES AND PROJECTS (OR "SEW WHAT"!)

CONCEPTS

- Hands-on experience is needed to perfect sewing skills.

OBJECTIVES

The student will:

- learn specific sewing skills and demonstrate his or her proficiency by completing sample sewing exercises
- complete a minimum of one sewing project using a kit or commercial pattern
- evaluate the completed sewing projects

TEACHER PREPARATION

- Determine the specific sewing skills students are to learn. For example, sew straight seams; be able to trim, grade, notch; to gather; to edge stitch; and so on.
- Select projects and patterns that include the skills identified above. Include a variety of projects so that students have a choice. The projects should vary from easy to moderately difficult.
- Type the list of acceptable projects and make copies for each student. Determine the date by which students must have made a choice and purchased their materials.
- Determine which techniques you are going to demonstrate to the students.
- Establish a calendar for student projects. How much time will be devoted to demonstration and student practice? How much time will students have to complete their projects?
- Make sure you have all of the materials students will need to complete the practice exercises.
- Cut fabric for practice exercises into 4″ x 8″ pieces.
- Make copies of the activity sheets "Sample Seam," "Staystitching," "Trim, Grade, Notch, and Clip," "Machine Basting or Gathering," and "Darts."
- Develop a system to provide help to students. You will frequently find several students will need help at the same time. One technique is to write HELP at the top of a chalkboard and the numbers 1 through 15 below. Have the students needing help write their name beside the next number. Erase the student's name when you have finished helping him or her.

● Select a sewing reference, such as *Teen Guide* by Valerie Chamberlain (New York: McGraw-Hill) or *Simplicity Sewing Book* (Simplicity Pattern Co., Inc., 200 Madison Avenue, New York, NY 10016). There are several editions of these books, and any edition will do.

ACTIVITIES

1. Demonstrate threading the sewing machine and winding the bobbin. Have the students practice these functions. Check to see if they can do them correctly. Have them practice sewing together some scraps of material.

2. Demonstrate pinning fabric and sewing a standard ⅝" seam. Include back stitching and pressing techniques in your demonstration. Distribute the activity sheet "Sample Seam," go over the directions, and have the students complete the practice exercise.

3. Demonstrate how to edge stitch a seam. Have students edge the seam they completed in the previous activity.

4. Explain and demonstrate staystitching. Distribute the activity sheet "Staystitching," explain the assignment, and let the students complete the practice exercise. Circulate around the room to make certain students are completing the exercise correctly.

5. Demonstrate how to trim, grade, notch, and clip a seam. Explain when and why each of these techniques would be used. Distribute the activity sheet "Trim, Grade, Notch, and Clip." Have the students answer the questions and then complete a sample of each technique. The sample should be pinned to a blank piece of paper, labeled, and submitted for review.

6. Demonstrate how to machine-gather using a basting stitch. Distribute the activity sheet "Machine Basting or Gathering" and review the directions for this procedure. Have students complete the activity sheet.

7. Demonstrate how to make a dart. Explain how it is to be pressed. Distribute the activity sheet "Darts." Have the students follow your directions to complete the activity.

8. Demonstrate any other techniques that students will need to complete their sewing projects.

9. Prepare the class for starting their projects. Go over the HELP process and any special rules you may have for your laboratory.

10. Involve the students in the evaluation of their projects. Offer suggestions for additional projects students may want to undertake. Consider displaying students' completed projects on a school bulletin board or in a display case.

SAMPLE SEAM

Materials Needed: scrap fabric, pins, thread, sewing machine set at 10–12 stitches per inch

Directions:

    a. Pin samples together (right sides together and edges matching).

    b. Stitch the seam on the seam line (5 guideline). Fasten both ends by backstitching about ½″.

    c. Clip off threads close to the fabric.

    d. Press seam open and flat.

    e. Answer the questions below by selecting the word from the boxed list that best completes the sentence. Write the word in the space provided.

    f. Staple your completed sample to this page and give it to your teacher.

stitching	cutting	raveling	open
right	match	guide	wrong

1. Stitch the seam on the _____ line.

2. To have the right side of the fabric showing in the finished garment, the _____ sides must be together when sewing.

3. To have a smooth-looking finished garment, press each seam _____ before crossing it with another seam.

SEAM SAMPLE EVALUATION:

Is the seam ⅝″ wide? _____

Is it sewn straight? _____

Is it backstitched at both ends? _____

What do you think your evaluation should be? _____

TEACHER EVALUATION:

_____

_____

_____

_____

_____

_____

_____

_____

STAYSTITCHING

Write the answers to the following questions as your teacher discusses and demonstrates staystitching.

1. What is staystitching? _____

_____

_____

2 Why is it done? _____

_____

_____

3. How far from the edge is it done? _____

4. How do you know you are stitching with the grain when you are staystitching? _____

_____

_____

_____

5. What stitch length is used for staystitching? _____

6. Follow your teacher's instructions to complete a practice staystitching sample.

 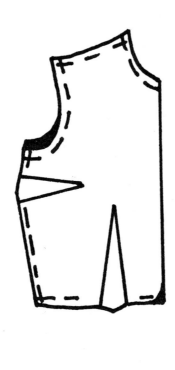 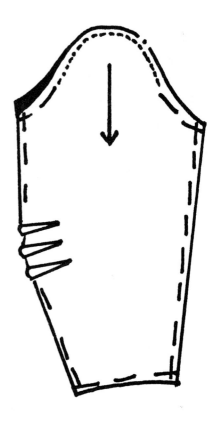

© 1990 by The Center for Applied Research in Education

TRIM, GRADE, NOTCH, AND CLIP

Your teacher will be explaining and demonstrating the finishing techniques of trimming, grading, notching, and clipping. Write the answers to the following questions in the spaces provided. This information will be helpful to you when you begin to work on your individual project.

1. What are two types of corners? _____

_____

_____

2. Make a drawing to indicate how each corner should be clipped. Label the corner type.

3. When might a seam be curved inward? _____

_____

4. When might a seam be curved outside? _____

_____

5. Do you clip or notch an inward curve? _____

6. Do you clip or notch an outward curve? _____

7. Why is grading done? _____

_____

_____

8. Complete your sample exercise.

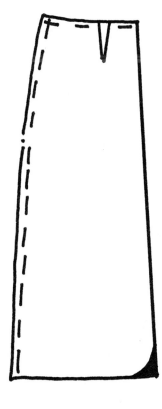

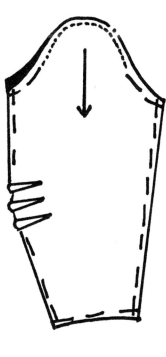

MACHINE BASTING OR GATHERING

A set of directions for machine basting or gathering is given below. You will have a sample exercise to complete after you have seen a demonstration. Watch the demonstration closely, and ask questions about anything you don't understand!

1. Use a basting stitch for machine gathering.

2. Do not back stitch when machine basting or gathering.

3. Put one row of stitches at ⅝″ from the edge and another row of stitches at ⅜″ from the edge. (See the illustration.)

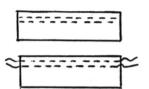

4. Leave a few inches of thread on each end to pull up the gathers. (See the illustration.)

5. Pull both bobbin threads to pull up the gathers.

6. Wrap the threads around a pin to secure the ends of the gathering. (See the illustration.)

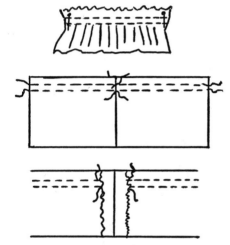

7. Divide the gathers into sections when gathering a long length of material. (See the illustration.)

8. To prevent breaking and to facilitate sliding gathers on long expanses of gathering, use buttonhole twist thread. (See the illustration.)

9. Set the stitch length dial back to 10–12 stitches per inch when finished basting or gathering.

10. When putting gathers in heavy or bulky fabrics, do not stitch through the seam allowance; only stitch up to them.

Now complete your practice exercise according to your teacher's directions.

DARTS

You are ready to practice stitching darts on a fabric sample. Watch your teacher demonstrate this process and follow instructions for completing your sample.

1. Use tracing paper and a tracing wheel to transfer the dart pictured below to a piece of fabric. Sew and press the dart.

2. Evaluation of sample:

    a. straight stitching _____

    b. tapered to a point _____   PIN COMPLETED

    c. back stitching at wide end _____   SAMPLE HERE!

    d. hand knot at narrow end _____

    e. flat pressing at narrow end _____

    f. neat appearance overall _____

3. Overall evaluation: _____

    _____

4. Transfer this dart:

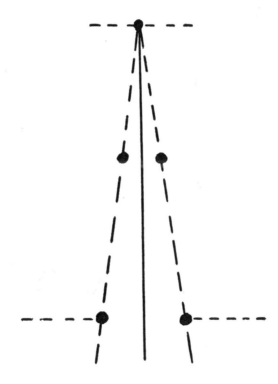

Appendix A

SAFETY SITUATION SCENARIO CARDS

SAFETY SITUATION 1

Sally was new in the cooking lab. She wanted to reach something on a shelf that was too high for her to reach from the floor. She chose a wobbly chair to stand on. It tipped when she stepped on it, she began to fall, and she bumped the handles of the saucepans that were on the stove.

1. What should Sally have chosen to stand on? Why?
2. How could Sally have prevented an accident with the saucepan handles?
3. Later, Sally used wet pot holders to remove a cake from the oven and burned her hands. What a bad day Sally was having! Why did her hands burn? What should she have done?

SAFETY SITUATION 2

You are heating fat in a frying pan when suddenly some of it spatters onto the burner of the stove. It catches on fire.

1. List the ways this fire could have been prevented. List as many as you can.
2. What would you do to extinguish a grease fire? Why?
3. If you had received a minor burn from the grease fire, what would you do? List the steps in the order in which they should be done.

SAFETY SITUATION 3

Pretend you are a home economics teacher. Explain the following information to your class:

1. When do you clean up spills?
2. How do you properly clean up and dispose of broken glass?
3. What are the reasons for keeping cupboard doors and drawers closed?
4. Describe the importance of pulling the oven rack from the stove before removing hot dishes or pans.

SAFETY SITUATION 4

The recipe you are using calls for chopping and peeling a lot of vegetables.

1. What surface should you use to chop the vegetables?
2. Describe the direction the blade of the knife should be moved in relation to yourself.
3. Which side of a knife blade would you use to scrape a cutting board? Why?
4. When and how should you wash sharp pieces of equipment?

SAFETY SITUATION 5

Pretend you are a home economics teacher. Explain the following information to your class:

1. Why must you never plug electrical appliances into an outlet when your hands are wet?
2. Why is it dangerous to have electrical cords dangling near dish water or other wet areas?
3. Describe the location of safety equipment in your classroom.

SAFETY SITUATION 6

You have been put in charge of an elementary school child who wants to make soup. The directions say to bring the soup to a boil. Tell how you would explain the following activities to the child:

1. How do you remove a lid from boiling food?
2. Why is it important to use the correct-size pan?
3. Why should you not stand with your back toward a lighted stove?

Appendix B

EVENTS IN TEXTILE HISTORY

EVENTS IN TEXTILE HISTORY

Prehistoric and Ancient Times

6300 B.C. . . . . Archaeological discovery of fine woven cloth fragments are found in Turkey; 30 to 38 threads per inch.

3000 B.C. . . . . Cotton is being grown in Pakistan, western India, and perhaps the Americas.

2700 B.C. . . . . Chinese cultivate silkworms and develop special looms to weave silk cloth.

2500 B.C. . . . . Linen is found on Egyptian mummy woven at 540 ends per inch, as well made as that of today. Goddess Isis is shown in a pictograph holding a shuttle.

327 B.C. . . . . Alexander the great is amazed at the beautiful printed cotton being produced in India.

300 B.C. . . . . Ancient Greeks and Romans develop an enormous trade in textiles.

75 B.C. . . . . Silk becomes the luxury cloth in Rome.

63 B.C. . . . . Cotton awnings are used in Rome.

The Middle Ages

400–1500 A.D. . . . . Textile industry gradually develops in Europe.

768 A.D. . . . . Charlemagne establishes silk-weaving industry at Lyons and imports wool from England.

900 A.D. . . . . Alfred the Great encourages expansion of the wool industry in England.

1120 . . . . Henry I sponsors the first woolen cloth guild. He relocates skilled Flemish weavers to English villages to increase production.

1153 . . . . First annual cloth fair is held in England.

1200 . . . . Spinning wheel is in common use.

1305 . . . . Venice has 17,000 people engaged in weaving wool.

1533 . . . . Pizarro reports that Peruvian spinning and weaving are superior to European.

1589 . . . . William Lee invents a machine to knit hosiery.

1631 . . . . Dutch East India Company imports fine calico from India.

Early 1600's . . . . Textile workers in the Netherlands develop imported methods of dyeing and finishing cloth.

1654 . . . . English textile craftsmen are forbidden to emigrate to America.

1661 . . . . A resident of Danzig, Poland builds a power loom. The government has him drowned and destroys the loom.

1667 . . . . English law requires all persons to be buried in woolen cloth. More cloth is being produced than can be sold.

1669 . . . . The English colonies in America are forbidden to trade in wool materials.

1696 . . . . Irish weavers produce cloth less expensively than the English. Attempts are made to suppress the weavers. Irish linen is superior to all others.

1733 . . . . John Kay, an Englishman, invents the flying shuttle loom.

1764 . . . . James Hargreaves invents the spinning jenny, the first machine to spin more than one piece of yarn at a time.

(continued)

Events In Textile History (continued)

1768	Spinning and weaving contests are held in America to oppose the Stamp Act.
1769	Richard Arkwright patents the water frame, a spinning machine that runs on water power.
1779	Samuel Crompton invents the spinning mule, a machine that combines the spinning jenny and the water frame.
1785	Edmund Cartwright patents the first power loom.
1790	Samuel Slater builds the first water-powered machine in the United States for spinning cotton.
1793	Eli Whitney invents the cotton gin.
1800	Ireland exports 25 million yards of woven linen.
1804	Jacquard loom uses punched cards to enable a single weaver to produce complex patterned fabric; an early example of computer technology.
1816	Power looms are beginning to be installed in large numbers in America.
1861	Union soldiers wear uniforms that are machine made; Confederate uniforms are still mostly made from handspun and handwoven fabric.
1884	Hilaire Chardonnet develops the first manufactured fiber, a form of rayon.
1900's	The Industrial Revolution completes sweeping the spinning and weaving processes from the home workshops to the factories and mills.
1910	Chardonnet's fiber is first produced in the United States under the name of artificial silk, now known as rayon.
1935	Wallace H. Carrothers develops nylon.
1940's to 1950's	Polyester, acrylic, and other artificial fibers are introduced.
1960's	Double-knit polyester fabric is introduced.
1970's	Knitting machines controlled by computers produce fabrics with highly complex patterns at tremendous speeds.
Early 1980's	Robots are introduced into the textile industry.
Late 1980's	Textile mills use high-speed looms that have many tiny shuttles called darts instead of a single shuttle. Other looms weave with no shuttles at all. A jet of water or air carries the filling through the warp up to 1000 times a minute—four times faster than a shuttle works on a standard high-speed loom.

Appendix C

ANSWER KEYS

FOODS AND NUTRITION

Safety

Answers will vary.

Kitchen Safety Quiz

1. dry pot holder or oven mitt
2. cup breaks from the heat of the water
3. in toward the center of
4. pull out the oven rack
5. they should be kept closed
6. away from yourself
7. several thicknesses of damp paper towels
8. wet
9. sturdy step stool

Experiment

Answers will vary.

Don't Be a Statistic

1. Bacteria are one-celled microorganisms that grow rapidly at room temperature.
2. 165°F
3. 40°F or below
4. improper storage and handling that lead to bacterial growth
5. Bacteria multiply rapidly once inside the human intestine.
6. Use clean utensils, keep your work area clean, and practice good personal hygiene. Don't eat food that smells bad.
7. It's split evenly.
8. five
9. Salmonella, Staphylococcus, Aureus (staph), Campylobacter Jejuni, Clostridium Perfringens, Clostridium Botulism
10. headaches, nausea, vomiting, cramps, dizziness, double-vision, flu-like symptoms, flatulence, and—in some cases—death

Sanitation Facts

1. True
2. True
3. d (all of the above)
4. Cook foods thoroughly to 165°F
5. By the word "EXP" or "Expiration Date"
6. Anything prepared with high-acid ingredients (i.e., vinegar and lemon juice); unblemished fresh fruit, raw vegetables, and "low moisture" low-fat cheeses
7. True
8. cooked vegetables
9. Yes, even longer if the food can be frozen.

10. Throw it away because salmonella can develop.
11. c (lead leaches into the juice)
12. a (40°F)
13. a. 1 day; b. 2 to 3 days; c. 4 to 5 weeks; d. 10 to 30 days; e. 3 to 4 days
14. in a half-full refrigerator, 1 day; in a full refrigerator, 2 days
15. b (0°F)
16. a (canned vegetables); b (cereals); e (dried fruit); f (soup); g (bouillon products)
17. True
18. Don't eat home-canned low-acid foods such as peas. Don't eat any food from a dented or bulging can.
19. It can cause an allergic reaction and respiratory problems.
20. False

A Measure of Success

1. a. Place liquid measuring cup on a level surface.
   b. Pour liquid up to the line indicating the correct measurement.
   c. Read the line at eye level.
2. a. Spoon ingredient lightly into a dry measuring cup.
   b. Do not pack unless the ingredient is shortening or brown sugar.
   c. Level with a straight-edged spatula.
3. Usually flour and confectioner's sugar because they need to be unpacked.
4. L—cranberry juice; L—water; H—cinnamon; H—cloves; L—lemonade; D—sugar; EQUIPMENT NEEDED—liquid measuring cup, saucepan, slotted spoon, wooden spoon, measuring spoons, straight-edged spatula, ladle; MY JOB(S)—answers will vary.

Did I Measure Up?

Answers will vary.

Tools of the Trade

1. Wooden spoon is used to stir hot foods on top of the stove and mix batters and doughs.
2. Slotted spoon is used to lift whole pieces of food from liquid.
3. Utility or two-tined fork is used to lift and turn large foods.
4. Ladle is used to serve hot beverages or soups.
5. Tongs are used to lift vegetables and meats from liquid or the pan, also to turn meats without piercing.
6. Pancake turner is used to lift or turn pancakes or other foods.
7. Rotary beater is used to beat icing, to beat eggs, or for whipping cream.

8. Wire whisk is used to beat air into egg whites or other liquid foods.
9. Electric mixer is used to mix cakes, cookies or other batters; it is also used to beat eggs and frostings.
10. Paring knife is used to pare or to cut vegetables and fruits.
11. Kitchen shears are used to trim pastry or to cut dried fruits.
12. Peeler is used to scrape or to peel vegetables.
13. Cutting board is used to protect the counter or tabletop when cutting or chopping.
14. Grater is used to grate cheese, vegetables, and some fruits.
15. Colander is used to strain coarse foods, to puree vegetables, or to separate liquid from pasta.
16. Sifter is used to unpack and aerate dry ingredients.
17. Measuring spoons are used to measure less than ¼ cup (or 65 ml) of any ingredient.
18. Liquid measuring cup is used to measure liquids.
19. Nested measuring cup is used to measure dry ingredients.
20. Straight-edged spatula is used to level dry ingredients or smooth icing.
21. Rubber scraper is used to scrape ingredients from bowls, pans, and measuring cups.
22. Pastry blender is used to cut in shortening into dry ingredients.
23. Pastry brush is used to grease pans, glaze baked products or meats and poultry.
24. Rolling pin is used to roll dough and pastry.
25. Pastry cloth is used to knead dough on or to roll out cookies and pastry on.

Muffins

UTENSILS NEEDED—dry measuring cups, spoon, straight-edged spatula, sifter, measuring spoons, liquid measuring cup, rubber scraper, muffin tin, 2 bowls, fork; MY JOB(S) ARE—Answers will vary.

Muffin Scorecard

Answers will vary.

Recipes Are Necessary

1. To get consistent food product quality; to know exactly which ingredients to use and their amounts; to know the exact mixing/blending procedure and the exact time and temperature for cooking.
2. To be sure you have the necessary ingredients and equipment; so you know if any prior preparation (i.e., chill overnight) is necessary; to see if you understand all cooking terms; to see if you have time to prepare the recipe before you want to serve it.
3. a. list of ingredients
   b. the procedure

4. Verbs (e.g., beat, sift, grease) in the recipe that indicate an action must be taken.
5. Read, assemble, collect, preheat, sifted, preheat, mix, cut in, add, stir, drop, greased, bake, remove, serve.
6. Action words are often the root word in the name of a utensil (i.e., sift/sifter, mix/mixer).
7. Some people have a special talent in the culinary field and, through practice, know when the right proportion of ingredients has been added. Some people make the same foods over and over and have, therefore, memorized the recipe. Some foods are simple to prepare and don't require a written set of directions.

Super Biscuits

UTENSILS NEEDED—sifter, spoon, dry measuring cups, straight-edge spatula, measuring spoons, liquid measuring cup, bowl, pastry blender, rubber scraper, fork, baking sheet, pancake turner, cooking rack, pot holders; MY JOB IS—Answers will vary.

What Did You Score

Answers will vary.

Microwave Magic

1. Microwaves are a form of electromagnetic energy much like that of heat, light, or radio waves.
2. A molecule is the smallest portion of an element or compound that retains chemical identity with the substance in mass.
3. Density refers to the lightness, firmness, or porous nature of a substance.
4. The microwaves penetrate the food and cause the molecules of the food to vibrate rapidly, thus creating heat.
5. Starting temperature, volume or amount of food, the density, moisture content, fat and sugar contents, and the shape of the food.
6. Pierce whole fruits or vegetables to allow steam to escape; do not cook eggs in the shell; pierce yolk with fork before cooking; allow steam to escape from plastic containers; stir liquids just before cooking; if foods smoke, turn off oven; do not use containers with small openings; do not pop regular popcorn (use microwaveable popcorn instead), do not use metal objects in the microwave; do not use newspaper and recycled paper in the microwave because they can burn.
7. Reduce the amount of liquid; add more thickening to sauces and gravies; reduce some seasonings; salt meat and vegetables after cooking; precook ingredients that take longer to microwave than others in the same dish.

Microwave Puzzle

Where Is It Hottest?

CONCLUSION—The outside edges of the foods will cook or get hot before the center of the food.

CONCLUSION—Foods with sugar and fat content will heat before those without the ingredients of sugar or fat.

Microwave vs. Conventional Cooking

Answers will vary.

Microwave vs. Conventional Cooking Scorecard

Answers will vary.

Technology Strikes Again!

1. They are foods that have been prepared so that part of the assembling, measuring, and mixing has been done in preparation for cooking. Part or all of the cooking may have been done.
2. Fresh, canned, frozen, dehydrated, partially prepared, ready-to-serve, and as packaged dry mixes.
3. Food additives are any ingredient added to the food during preparation, processing, or packaging for an intentional purpose (i.e., to add color, to improve shelf life).
4. They are added to improve or protect the color, flavor, and texture, and to retain the nutritive value of foods.
5. Generally yes, if they are used in small quantities. Some food additives are unsafe or of questionable safety (e.g., Red Color #2, #3, #4, #40, carbon black, cyclamates, saccharin, sodium nitrate).
6. Convenience foods generally save time and energy, but you should also consider the cost, quality, nutritive value, and your skill in food preparation.
7. The cost of processing, packaging, labor and management, shipping, and marketing.
8. If you want to spend less time preparing food; if your preparation skills are weak; if you have limited equipment, supplies or ingredients; or if you wish to use a convenience food to create variety in menus.
9. The cook still needs to interpret cooking terms, know heat principles, and be able to follow directions.

I Wonder What It is

Answers will vary.

Compare

Answers will vary in the comparison chart.

1. Culture, special diet, availability, cost
2. Fresh food is available from a distance of thousands of miles; we have a wider choice of food products; food products can be partially prepared or fully prepared and ready for consumption.
3. The ingredients in convenience foods may not be the same kind and in the same proportion as those in homemade products. There can be a difference in nutritive values.
4. The mixing techniques to be followed in a packaged mix; heat principles must be followed; procedures must be followed in correct sequence; when working with dough, do not overmix or handle if pastry, and knead properly if making bread.
5. Time available; equipment available; skill level.

Personal Energy Estimate

Answers will vary.

Nutrient Knowledge

Protein	For energy, growth, repair, and synthesis of tissues	meat, fish, poultry, eggs, milk, cheese, dried beans
Carbohydrates	Energy	fruits, vegetables, breads, cereals

Fat	Energy	cream, whole milk, oil, salad dressings, meats, butter
B Vitamins	Regulates appetite, nervous system, ... and contributes to complexion	milk products, bread and cereal products
Vitamin A	Helps keep skin healthy, and helps .... eyes adjust to darkness	deep yellow fruits and vegetables, leafy greens
Vitamin C	Heals bruises, promotes healthy gums	citrus fruits, strawberries, green vegetables
Calcium and Phosphorus	Builds strong bones and teeth	milk and dairy products
Iron	For red blood cells, carries oxygen .... throughout the body	liver, meat, leafy greens, bread and cereal
Water	Part of every cell, it carries .... nutrients to cells and removes waste	water, fruits, vegetables, juices, soups, milk

Dietary Recall

Answers will vary.

Diet Evaluation

Answers will vary.

Menu Plan

Answers will vary.

HUMAN GROWTH AND DEVELOPMENT

Play Inventory

Part I

1. F	9. T
2. F	10. F
3. T	11. T
4. T	12. F
5. T	13. T
6. T	14. F
7. F	15. F
8. T	

Part II

1. P	7. P, E
2. M	8. E
3. P, E	9. M, E
4. S	10. P, S, M
5. S	11. S
6. M	12. S

Part III

Answers will vary. Here are points that students might make: Play helps a child get rid of feelings of aggression and provides an outlet for excess energy. It's a way for a child to find out about the world and an opportunity for self-discovery. Play helps to develop all parts of the body as well as to develop abilities the child will use all through life (i.e., getting along with others, opportunities to share/give/take/cooperate, and opportunities to conform to rules). Play contributes to the development of self-concept, keen senses, problem solving abilities, and a way for children to think about new ideas.

Child's Play

1. a. social, mental
    b. physical, emotional
    c. mental
    d. mental, social
    e. physical, emotional
2–5. Answers will vary.

Types of Play Activities

1. From the simple act of participating in the activity: satisfaction is intrinsic or inherent in the activity itself.
2. Runs, climbs, explores, constructs, participates in dramatic play
3. By being entertained or amused by watching what someone else does

4. Listening to music, stories, conversation; by watching others (children, adults, animals, or activities others are involved in); looking at books, pictures, TV, movies, videos

5. Solitary play is presocial play. The child does not interact with others. Looking at a crib mobile or watching his or her own hands are examples.

6. Children who play alongside other children, but do not interact with the other children, are engaging in parallel play. Stacking blocks or building sand castles by yourself are examples.

7. Children become interested in playing with each other, usually in small groups of two or three. Generally, they will build something together or determine an organized way to line up stuffed animals, etc.

8. This is group play, with the group becoming larger. There is interest by members of the group in understanding and completing the activity. A ball game or constructing a project are examples.

9. solitary; parallel

10. cooperative; associative

11. Give children time to explore and try out new things; help children with scissors, swings, and tools; show safe methods to use materials; don't allow children near equipment that might be harmful; keep group size small; teach basic rules for safety (i.e., don't throw sand); do not allow one child to monopolize a popular toy; allow children to learn by doing; do not distinguish between "boy" and "girl" toys; do not participate in the play too much yourself; do not teach children to play to win because they need to experience the process of play.

Toy Selection

SAFETY: Avoid hard edges, sharp plastic; look for the words "non-toxic" and "non-flammable" on labels. Avoid small detachable parts until you know children can use them safely. Wooden equipment should be free from splinters. Play areas should have adequate space and wheel toys should have a large base to prevent spills.

CONSTRUCTION: Materials should be sturdy and durable. Outdoor equipment should withstand weathering, materials should be suitable for the purposes intended. Toys should be washable if used in water. Wooden equipment should be screwed together, not glued, and be of hard wood. Materials should be warm and pleasant to touch.

PURPOSE: The toy should be appropriate for its intended purpose—the physical, mental, social, or emotional development of the child.

APPEARANCE: The toy should look like what it is meant to be, but be free from unnecessary detail. If unfamiliar, the toy should clarify concepts rather than confuse the child. The toy should be aesthetically pleasing in shape, color, and feel.

DESIGN: It should be scaled to the child's size. The toy should be adaptable so children can use their own imaginations. Parts that move should work. The design should be simple so the toy can be used without elaborate explanation.

COST: Expense should be related to the durability of the item and the extent to which it will be used. Sturdy toys are more economical than fragile ones.

Toys for a Purpose

ACTIVE PHYSICAL PLAY: push and pull toys, wheel toys, sports, gym equipment

MANIPULATIVE, CONSTRUCTIVE, CREATIVE PLAY: blocks, construction tools, drawing and painting equipment, hobby kits, puzzles, clay

IMITATIVE, IMAGINATIVE, DRAMATIC PLAY: dolls, housekeeping equipment, large boxes, train systems, dress-up costumes

SOCIAL PLAY: games in which several children can take part, tea parties, organized fun

Toys for Different Ages

INFANCY TO TWO YEARS: They like brightly colored, lightweight toys of varied textures. Toys should be washable, too big to swallow, free from sharp corners and rough edges. Examples are stuffed animals, dolls, push and pull toys, blocks, large take-apart beads, bath toys, things to bite/shake/pound/bang/pour.

TWO TO FOUR YEARS: They need toys for more active play, such as push, pull, and pedal toys, and cars and trucks big enough to straddle. Also, they need animals on wheels, wheelbarrows, doll carriages, things to climb, party sets, cooking equipment, stuffed animals, chalk, crayons, puzzles, paints, trains, planes, autos, trucks, picture books, records, and small set of table and chairs.

FOUR TO SIX YEARS: This age group still needs active play—gym equipment, low bars, rings, climbing apparatus, slides, swings, tumbling mats for large muscles and wagons, tricycles, wheel toys, and sleds for winter. This group needs simple construction toys and puzzles for manipulative skills and motor skills. Children need block sets with more sizes and shapes, along with trains, trucks, planes, cranes, boats, and cars to use with blocks as well as farm animals, zoo animals, and circus toys. Tractors, ditch diggers, hammers and nails, paints, clay, modeling sets, easy weaving and sewing equipment, paper, blunt scissors, paste, stick-ons, dolls, doctor/nurse kits, equipment to play store and equipment for community activities (firefighters, letter carriers), simple games, books, and musical instruments are all appropriate.

How Old Am I?

1. a. 4 to 6 years old
   b–c. Answers will vary.
2. a. infant to 2 years old
   b–c. Answers will vary.
3. a. 2 to 4 years old
   b–c. Answers will vary.

Observations

1–6. Answers will vary.

What Do You Know About Toy Safety?

1. False. The variety of toys on the market is staggering and some of the hazards in toys are not immediately observable.
2. False. U.S. Consumer Product Safety Commission estimates over 170,000 people were treated in hospital emergency rooms for toy-associated injuries; many more were treated in doctors' offices.
3. False. Some stuffed toys have small parts that can be removed, swallowed, or inhaled by a small child. Some are constructed with wires supporting arms and legs.
4. False. They become dangerous because glass, metal, or brittle plastic parts become sharp edges that can cut or stab. Small pieces can be swallowed or inhaled.
5. True. Labels recommend toys for specific ages. Labels also list non-toxic on painted toys or flame-resistant on fabric toys.
6. True. They can be too advanced for the physical development, skill, and coordination of the child. A child may not have the proper strength or balance to use the toy safely. Some toys frustrate a child.
7. False. Putting toys on shelves or in boxes prevents accidents. Stepping on toys or falling over them can cause serious injuries.
8. False. Any toy can be dangerous if misused. Children can be taught the safe way to use toys. Requiring safety still leaves room for creativity.
9. False. Although children's play should be generally supervised, particularly the under-six group, realistically this cannot be done 100% of the time. Therefore, toys should be as hazard-free as possible.
10. True. They ban toys and other articles intended for use by children that present an electrical, mechanical, or thermal hazard.
11. False. The U.S. Consumer Product Safety Commission cannot dictate how a toy will be used nor does it get to inspect toys in the stores after they have been manufactured. The commission does not determine age levels for toys, the manufacturer does.

12. True. Specific skills can be taught depending on the age of the child, but supervision is needed to prevent the possibility of injury.

Toy Evaluation

1–8. Answers will vary.

Draft Guidelines for Toy Selection

Answers will vary.

Recommended Toy Selection Guidelines

Answers will vary.

Evaluation of a Children's Book

Answers will vary.

Storytelling Evaluation Checklist

Answers will vary.

Self-Evaluation

Answers will vary.

Foods for Children

1. breast milk; formula
2. cereals, fruits/vegetables, meats and protein foods, finger foods, table foods
3. Serve at least three different colors at each meal; i.e., orange carrots, green salad, and brown hamburger. Serve flavor contrasts; i.e., turkey and cranberries, or grilled cheese sandwich and a pickle. To add texture, have one soft food, one chewy food, and one crisp food at each meal; i.e., tossed salad, macaroni and cheese, and a cookie for dessert.
4. Have suitably sized tables and chairs so that the child's feet will rest on the floor. Provide plates, cups, and eating utensils that can be managed by small hands. Provide a bright, well-ventilated and clean eating area.
5. Do not make an issue over the child's appetite. Provide a casual relaxed atmosphere. Schedule meals for a regular time each day. Remove the food from the table if the child dawdles. Accept occasional accidents as a part of the learning process.
6. Don't force the issue if certain foods are rejected. Encourage trying new foods even if it is only a taste. Permit temporary excesses of eating or rejecting certain foods. Permit self-feeding even if messy. Provide adult conversation about food.

A Nutritious Snack

Answers will vary.

Characteristics of Three- and Four-Year-Olds

PHYSICAL: This age child can run, jump, hop, skip, gallop, and climb. The child can march to rhythm and execute dancing motions. He or she can roll and crawl on the floor, and balance self on one foot. This age group can pedal wheel toys; touch toes, do sit-ups, chin-ups, and push-ups; can throw and bounce a ball, catch a ball or beanbag; string beads; build with blocks; cut with scissors; use large crayons and pencils; fold paper; screw and unscrew objects; scribble and draw directed lines; manipulate puzzles; build a tower; manipulate fork or spoon; and dress with success except for tying bows and fastening buttons.

EMOTIONAL: Children of this age group are usually affectionate, especially to sibling and caring adults. They are now switching emotional dependence on the family to emotional dependence on other children or on adults outside of the family. Negative behaviors are usually expressed by aggressive behavior or open hostility. Some children express negative feelings in a passive, quiet manner.

MENTAL: This age child can imitate, pretend, and show insight. Three- and four-year-olds have language abilities and progress to more complex thinking; however, they have difficulty in mentally putting themselves in place of another person. A child this age recognizes and counts objects that are similar, but he or she does not have the ability to arrange and rearrange objects in an organized logical manner. This age child believes the experiences of the moment.

SOCIAL: This age child can cooperate with others and exhibit independence. Three- and four-year-olds are ready to learn to conform to standards, make contributions, appreciate traditions, and interact with others.

Am I Three or Am I Four?

1. 3	10. 4
2. 4	11. 4
3. 4	12. 3
4. 3	13. 3
5. 3	14. 4
6. 4	15. 4
7. 3	16. 3
8. 4	17. 4
9. 3	18. 4

Plan of Action

Answers will vary.

What Did I See?

Answers will vary.

MANAGEMENT AND CONSUMERISM

Making Your Own Decision

Answers will vary.

Making Your Choice

1–8. Answers will vary.

Advertising Appeals

Answers will vary.

Finding the "Hooks"

Answers will vary.

Write a Jingle

Answers will vary.

Time to Research a Product

Answers will vary.

My Report

Summaries will vary.

Consumer Product Survey

Answers will vary.

Product Comparisons

Answers will vary.

Energy Costs

Part I:
Transport to processing plant
*Prepare in processing plant and package
Keep frozen in storage and during transportation
Keep frozen in store until the consumer buys it
Continue to freeze until the consumer is ready to eat it
*Manufacture the box or bag and prepare a label
Use energy to drive to the store and purchase the french fries
Heat the french fries to be eaten

Part II:
Yes. You pay for each step of transportation, processing, packaging, and storage.

Environmental Impact

Part I:
burger in plastic foam container—Never
fries in paper bag—2.5 months
plastic container for beverage and straw—50 to 80 years
plastic container and spoon for ice cream sundae—50 to 80 years

Part II:

Yes. The range of time for the containers to decompose is 2.5 months to never.

Part III:

Answers will vary.

Costs Compared

1. A; more of the menu items were transported, processed, and stored in a freezer.
2. A; the consumer pays for the costs associated with transporting, processing, and storing food.
3. B; my skill level and/or time available were adequate or if I had cooking utensils.
4. B; the food has not had nutrients processed out during cooking due to high temperatures being used.
5. A
6. A; of transportation, fuel, packaging, processing, and reheating costs.
7. more (1061); protein, calcium, vitamins A and B, iron, fat, and carbohydrates as leader
8. fewer (685); protein, calcium, vitamins A, B, C, iron, and carbohydrates as leader
9. B. There is less processing, packaging, and storage before it reaches the consumer.

Personal Costs

1. convenience foods, packaging, transportation, storage, and reheating costs
2. the cost of going to the store to purchase the food and refrigerating it
3. Answers will vary.
4. B; he or she used a tablecloth and napkins, lots of dishes, ran hot water and used the dishwasher. However, his or her environmental costs were lower when the cost to decompose litter such as plastic utensils is considered.

5–6. Answers will vary.

Summarizing

Answers will vary.

How to Get Action

1. carefully; briefly
2. when; where; item; service
3. defective
4. style numbers; catalog numbers; order numbers; brand; price
5. steps; solve the problem
6. claim
7. copies; receipts
8. copy
9. second; copy; first
10. last; another
11. next; who
12. return; inside or business; salutation; body; complimentary; name (signature)

The Rewrite

Rewrites will vary.

One More Time

Letters will vary.

It's Not Over 'Till It's Over

Answers will vary.

TEXTILES AND CLOTHING

Ten Top Events in the History of Textiles

Answers will vary.

Clothing Production—Then and Now

1. clothing industry
2. factory
3. speed
4. spinning
5. weaving
6. metal needles
7. Isaac Singer
8. treadle-powered
9. hands
10. machine
11. band knife
12. layers
13. cloth
14. lasers
15. fold
16. cutting table
17. buttonhole
18. buttons
19. pressing
20. iron
21. Boston
22. 1800's
23. sailors
24. clothes
25. secondhand
26. demand
27. tailors
28. ties
29. stockings
30. Boston

31. New York City
32. Philadelphia
33. Cincinnati
34. cutting
35. sewing
36. journeyman tailors
37. hand
38. sewing machine
39. 1851
40. revolutionized
41. 900
42. 30 to 40
43. factories
44. immigrants
45. 19th
46. apartments
47. sewed
48. Civil War
49. uniforms
50. assembly
51. skills
52. Standardized
53. men's wear
54. women
55. children
56. underwear
57. silk kimonos
58. shirtwaists
59. immigrants
60. sweatshops
61. 14 to 18
62. $14
63. $4
64. Triangle Shirtwaist Factory
65. garment
66. pay
67. working hours
68. working conditions
69. World War II
70. benefit programs
71. retirement pay
72. Seventh Avenue
73. workrooms
74. showrooms
75. piece-goods
76. small section
77. reduced
78. piece
79. designers
80. Paris
81. clothing
82. fashion design

83. manufacturing
84. brand names
85. manufacture
86. design
87. distribute
88. domestic
89. foreign
90. computer
91. CAD
92. patterns
93. Robots
94. memories
95. 1970's
96. overseas
97. countries
98. lower
99. India
100. Pakistan
101. Sri Lanka
102. Hong Kong
103. South Korea
104. Taiwan
105. China
106. importers
107. less
108. less
109. negotiated
110. 1980's
111. importing
112. ten
113. exporting

From Fabric to Garment

Designer chooses fabric swatches.
Designer prepares sketch.
Fabric and colors are chosen.
Sample garment is made up.
Cost sheet detailing expenses for fabric, trimmings, labor, and shipping expenses is prepared.
Wholesale price is calculated.
Production pattern is created and graded for size range.
Marker is made.
Fabric is laid out in multiple layers and cut by machine.
Cut goods are bundled and sent to sewing room.
Cut goods are assembled.
Assembled garments are inspected, pressed, packed, or hung on racks, and shipped to retailer.

Pluses and Minuses

ADVANTAGES: lower cost, greater selection, require less care, increased standardization

DISADVANTAGES: loss of jobs in the U.S. garment industry, negative effect on the trade deficit, many garments poorly constructed, increased standardization had led to a reduction in sizes available

Characteristics of Fabrics

DURABILITY: Refers to resistance to wear

PERMANENT PRESS: Special finish to keep garment smooth, wrinkle-free, and to reduce shrinkage

SOIL RETARDANT: Special finish to keep dirt from attaching to a fabric

ANTISTATIC: Treatment to garment to prevent static cling, especially of undergarments

WATER REPELLENT: Special finish to make fabric repel water

ANTI-SHRINKING: Treatment to fabric after it is made to limit shrinkage to no more than 3%

COLORFAST: Color is set during dyeing so that it will not run when washed

SOFT: Surface of smooth fabrics are napped to give them a soft airy look

A Guide to Fibers

COTTON	batiste; broadcloth; corduroy; denim; seersucker; terry	versatile and durable; withstands frequent washing; irons easily at high temperature
LINEN	damask; handerchief; nubby texture	withstands frequent washing; does not shed lint; wrinkles easily unless treated; resists dye-type stains; more expensive than cotton
SILK	broadcloth; chiffon; crepe de chine; linen; raw silk	strong with natural lustre; resists wrinkling; more expensive than synthetic silky yarns
WOOL	challis; crepe; flannel; gabardine; jersey	retains shape; requires little pressing; has versatility in fabrics; has insulating capacity
ACETATE	satin; silk-like fabrics; taffeta; tricot	drapes well; dries quickly; subject to fume-fading; inexpensive
ACRYLIC	double-knits; fleece knits; pile fabrics; wool-like fabrics	completely washable; resists stretching and shrinking; nonabsorbant; quick to dry; resists wrinkling; resistant to effects of sun
NYLON	tricot; two-way stretch; velvet; wet-look cire	completely washable; resists stretching and shrinking; easy to wash—quick to dry; nonabsorbant; retains shape
POLYESTER	cotton-, silk- and wool-like fabrics; crepe; double and single knit; gabardine; jersey	completely washable; resists stretching and shrinkage; nonabsorbant; easy to wash—quick to dry; sharp pleat and crease retention
RAYON	challis; linen-like fabrics; matte jersey	is absorbant; lacks resilience and wrinkles easily; is flammable; inexpensive

Strengths and Weaknesses of Natural and Synthetic Fibers

COTTON	comfortable; soft; sturdy; "breathes"; inexpensive	wrinkles easily; mildews; must be treated to be flame resistant
LINEN	comfortable; "breathes"; lint free; durable; resists heat/ moths/perspiration damage	wrinkles easily; does not hold a crease; expensive; flammable
SILK	soft; smooth; drapes well; comfortable; luxurious feel; wrinkle resistant	does not keep crease, weakened by heat and perspiration, yellows from age and sunlight
WOOL	absorbant; colorfast; warm; resists wrinkles; durable; not flammable	pills; not moth resistant; usually requires dry cleaning
ACRYLIC	some wool-like qualities; soft and warm; retains shape; not damaged by sun; dries quickly	pills; does not "breathe"; not strong; flammable; holds static electricity
NYLON	very strong but lightweight; silky and stretchable; does not shrink; resists mildew and moths	does not "breathe"; pills; wrinkles; damaged by sunlight; burns and melts at high temperatures
POLYESTER	machine wash and dry; resists wrinkling; strong; resists mildew and moths	difficult to remove oily stains; does not "breathe"; can be scratchy
RAYON	blends well with other fibers; "breathes"; economical	wrinkles; mildews; does not hold shape well

What's Best for What?

Answers will vary.

How Do I Take Care of It?

MACHINE WASH—wash, bleach, dry, and press by a customary method including commercial laundering and dry cleaning

HOME LAUNDER ONLY—same as above, but no commercial laundering

NO BLEACH—do not use any type of bleach

COLD WASH/COLD RINSE—use cold water from faucet of cold water machine setting

WARM WASH/WARM RINSE—use warm water from faucet or warm water machine setting

NO SPIN—remove before final machine spin cycle

HAND WASH—launder only by hand in lukewarm water; may be bleached and dry cleaned

WASH SEPARATELY—wash alone or with like colors

DELICATE/GENTLE CYCLE—use appropriate machine setting or wash by hand

TUMBLE DRY—dry in tumble dryer at specific heat setting (high, medium, low, or no heat)

TUMBLE DRY/REMOVE PROMPT—same as tumble dry, but if no cool-down cycle, remove as soon as tumbling stops

DRIP DRY—hang wet and allow to dry with hand shaping only

LINE DRY—hang damp and allow to dry

NO WRING/TWIST—hang dry, drip dry, or dry flat; handle to prevent wrinkles and stretching

DRY FLAT—lay garment on flat surface to dry

BLOCK TO DRY—maintain original size and shape while drying

COOL IRON—set iron at lowest setting

WARM IRON—set iron at medium setting

HOT IRON—set iron at hot setting

DO NOT IRON—do not iron or press with heat

STEAM IRON—iron or press with steam

IRON DAMP—dampen garment before ironing

DRY CLEAN ONLY—garment should be dry cleaned only, including self-service

PROFESSIONAL DRY CLEAN—do not use self-service dry cleaning

NO DRY CLEAN—use recommended care instructions; do not use any dry-cleaning substances

Points to Consider

1. Fabric—Should be appropriate for the silhouette and structural design of the garment. It should be suitable for the intended use of the garment.
2. Grainline—All pieces of a garment should be cut on the grainline of the fabric; if they are not, the garment will not fit comfortably or hang as it should.
3. Plaids, checks, stripes—Should be matched at openings, seams, collars, cuffs, and pockets.
4. Fabric with pile or nap—Should be cut in one direction.
5. Interfacing, lining, underlining—Should be suitable in weight, crispness, color, and care characteristics for fabric and style of the garment.
6. Top-stitching—Should be straight and an even distance from an edge.
7. Darts—Should be symmetrical on both sides of the garment and fit the body contour. They should taper gradually to a point.
8. Gathering—Should be neat and even, with the fullness evenly distributed.
9. Seams—Should be smooth, free of puckering, true in line, and uniform in width. Enclosed seams should be trimmed and graded to reduce bulk.
10. Collars—Both ends of a collar should be equal in shape, length, and distance from the center of the garment.
11. Set-in sleeves—The cap of the sleeve should have a smooth roll without puckers or gathers. The armhole should be smooth and true to line. The seam allowance of an armhole should be turned toward the sleeve.
12. Hems—Should be smooth, inconspicuous, and even in width.
13. Plackets—Should be neat and flat with sufficient lap to avoid gapping.
14. Zippers—Should be entirely covered by fabric unless exposed as part of the design. They should not buckle or make the placket pucker.
15. Buttonholes—The color of the thread should match the color of the fabric unless the buttonholes are used for decorative design.
16. Buttons—There should be enough space under the button for fastening the garment without pull on the fabric.
17. Belts, waistbands—Should be firm enough so they will not roll when worn.
18. Pressing—The garment should be free of wrinkles. There should be no shine from overpressing. There should be no seam, dart, or hem imprints on the right side of the garment. Vertical darts should be pressed toward the center of the garment while horizontal darts are pressed downward.

A Question of Quality

Answers will vary.

Color Theory

1. red, yellow, green, blue, purple
2. a. Means color. It is the quality that distinguishes one color from another. For example, red from blue.
   b. Value is the quality of lightness or darkness found in a color. For example, light blue from dark blue.
   c. Chroma is the quality of brightness or dullness of a color. For example, pink from dusty pink or rose.
   d. Undertone describes the color you get when you take the five basic hues and add either blue or yellow to them. For example, blue/red, yellow/green.
   e. Pigment is the coloring matter in cells and tissues.
   f. Melanin is any of the various dark pigments of animal origin, as that of dark-complexioned people.
3. winter, spring, summer, fall (autumn)
4. your skin, your eyes, and your hair; skin is most important
5. blue
6. yellow
7. a. WINTER: *skin*—white, light to deep rose-beige, light to dark olive, black, brown-black, brown; *eyes*—light to dark brown, black-brown, blue-grey, yellow-green, turquoise, dark blue, violet, hazel; *hair*—platinum blonde to golden blonde, medium to dark brown, black-brown, grey (silver)
   b. SUMMER: *skin*—fair with delicate pink tone, light to medium rose-beige, deep rose beige; *eyes*—clear blue or grey-blue, clear green or grey-green, aquamarine, hazel, soft cool brown; *hair*—light ash blonde, medium ash blonde, light to medium ash brown, dark ash brown, grey (silver)
   c. SPRING: *skin*—ivory, golden ivory, pink or peach, deep peach, light to medium beige, rosy glow; *eyes*—light to dark blue, blue-grey, green-blue aqua, gold-green, light gold-brown, topaz-yellow; *hair*—flaxen blonde, golden blonde, strawberry blonde, light to dark brown, grey, white
   d. AUTUMN: *skin*—ivory, light peach, medium peach, deep peach, light beige, medium beige, dark beige, florid; *eyes*—light to dark brown, red-brown, olive-brown, golden-green, hazel, turquoise; *hair*—honey blonde, strawberry blonde, bright red to deep auburn, light to dark brown with gold or red highlights, deep chestnut brown, white (warm)

Color and You

Answers will vary.

Line and Design

1. A wardrobe is a collection of clothing that makes it possible to carry out daily activities in a satisfactory manner.

2. Climate, activities, comfort, involvement in sports
3. It is a principle that can be applied to any situation where you want to create an attractive design. For example: table-setting, gardening, food presentation, gift-wrapped packages, store displays, etc.
4. rhythm, balance, emphasis, proportion
5. *proportion/scale:* how the body is divided; unequal divisions of space equal more interest
   balance: symmetrical balance is when both sides or parts are equal; asymmetrical balance is when each side does not look like the other, but lines and color give balance to the garment
   emphasis: is a highlight in design, or a center of interest; it is usually done by contrasts in color, texture, or unusual shape
   rhythm: the orderly way line, color, and texture have been arranged so that your eye moves easily from one part of the design to another
6. color, line, texture
7. They can improve the appearance of body proportions, accent certain traits, improve personal image. They can make a slim body appear larger, or de-emphasize body size.
8. daily activity, sports involvement, the climate where you live, how comfortable you like to be, design principles, and the elements of clothing design

Wardrobe—A Blueprint for Success!

Answers will vary.

The Conventional Sewing Machine

1. stitch pattern dial
2. tension dial
3. self-threading take-up lever
4. tension disks
5. presser foot
6. feed
7. needle or throat plate
8. spool pins
9. bobbin winder
10. hand wheel
11. needle position dial
12. stitch width dial
13. stitch control dial
14. reverse stitch control
15. needle clamp

The Principle Parts

1. the control that allows for a variety of stitch lengths
2. holds fabric against feed
3. controls the flow of the needle thread
4. selects the right tension for the stitch, thread, and fabric being used
5. secured by magnets, it lifts out for removal; guidelines on right and left sides help keep seams straight
6. controls the movement of the take-up lever and the needle
7. places the needle in either the left, center, or right stitching position
8. instantly reverses the stitching direction
9. holds spools of various sizes for threading the machine and winding the bobbin
10. controls the width of zigzag stitching and positions the needle for straight stitching
11. turns on the machine and sewing light simultaneously
12. helps fill the bobbin quickly
13. eliminates the possibility of inserting the needle backwards
14. allows the presser foot to be raised or lowered
15. opens to expose the bobbin
16. controls the speed of the machine
17. moves the fabric under the presser foot
18. regulates the amount of tension on the needle thread

The Computerized Sewing Machine

1. chart with preprogrammed stitches
2. automatic buttonhole
3. automatic needle position
4. electronic bobbin thread monitor
5. automatic needle threader
6. dual feed
7. automatic tie-off
8. presser foot
9. flat-bed free arm
10. spool pins (not visible)
11. digital display
12. memory
13. needle position
14. display key
15. reverse stitching

Questions

1. The main difference is the digital display and push buttons to select computerized functions on the high-tech machine; otherwise, they are similar.
2. The computerized machine is controlled by a microprocessor with a silicon chip. Conventional sewing machines operate from mechanical parts driven by a motor.
3. If you did a lot of sewing, such as creating designs and having them sewn on fabric, or if you worked with very delicate fabrics.
4. Sewing simple seams, mending, craft projects, and general household sewing of commercial patterns.

Comparing the Features

Conventional Machine: ADVANTAGES—lower cost, easy to use, with attachments it can buttonhole, hem, and sew on buttons, can change stitches from straight to zigzag, can do embroidery stitches and monogramming; DISADVAN-TAGES—does not have memory so stitch length dials must be turned by hand, you must back-stitch or tie off threads manually at the end of a seam, you must manually turn the wheel to put the needle in the up position at the end of a seam, does not warn you when bobbin thread is low

High-Tech Machine: ADVANTAGES—scans your own embroidery designs and sews them, preprogrammed stitches and automatic buttonholes are in memory bank, it has utility programs from darning to mending to sewing on buttons to sewing buttonholes, needle automatically goes to the up position when you finish a seam, sews through 12 layers of fabric (dual feed), automatically ties off seams, monitor warns you when you are low on bobbin thread; DISADVANTAGES—higher price tag; learning to use a computerized machine and its specialized vocabulary; you may have a machine that does much more than you need a machine to do; computerized machines do not like cold temperatures so the room needs to be warm

READING THE PATTERN

1. notch
2. the seamline
3. dots to match seams
4. arrows to indicate sewing direction
5. dart
6. buttonhole
7. center fold line
8. grainline
9. lines to lengthen or shorten garment

Pattern Markings

```
                    C
                    L
          E A S I N G          C
          R   P   R            O
    S     R   G A T H E R I N G
P L E A T S   O   I            S
A   A       W     N            T
T   M   D O T S   L            R
T   L   A         I            U
E   I   R         N            C
R   N O T C H E S E            T
N   E S     Q                  I
            L                  O
        M A R K I N G S         N
            D
B U T T O N H O L E S
            I
            N
            E
            S
```

Sample Seam

1. ⅝″
2. right
3. open

Answers to the evaluation will vary.

Staystitching

1. It is a line of regular machine stitching done on the curved edges of a garment.
2. It is done to hold the fabric grain on bias or curved edges so that these edges will not stretch during the construction of the garment.
3. The line of stitching is made ½″ from the cut edge with matching thread, through a single thickness of the seam allowance.
4. The grainline will be marked by arrows to indicate the directions on your "Cutting and Sewing Direction Sheet."
5. 2.5

Trim, Grade, Notch, and Clip

1. inside corner, outside corner
2.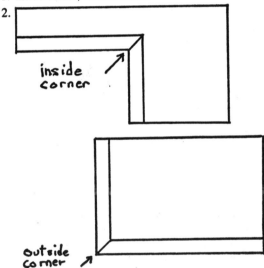

3. armhole
4. collar
5. clip
6. notch
7. To reduce the bulk of fabric at the seam line

Darts

Answers will vary.